Go forth and do good,

Randy Lisk

The
Clark
Group

Lexington, Kentucky

The
PAGE

10 POWERFUL IDEAS TO
TRANSFORM ANY BUSINESS

Lisk Associates

3244 Brenheim Way | Lexington, KY 40503-3474

www.liskassociates.com | randy@liskassociates.com

ISBN 978-1-883589-88-2

Designed by Kelly Elliott

ACKNOWLEDGEMENTS

"If you want to make an apple pie from scratch, you must first create the universe."
— CARL SAGAN

This quote from Carl Sagan, the American astronomer and astrophysicist, came to mind when I began thinking about how to acknowledge those who helped create this book "from scratch." All things, including this book, are created from previous causes and conditions. Those things came from yet other causes and conditions. How can I write an acknowledgement to include all those innumerable instances and people in my life, both major and minor, that led to this book without leaving someone out? Here is a class-action acknowledgement to all of you — past and present, family, teachers, clients, friends and strangers — who through some interaction influenced me and therefore helped me write this book. I appreciate all of you, even those I have never met.

Having said that, there are a few indispensable causes and conditions that must be recognized. I'd like to thank my long-time friend and collaborator, Jon Nipple, for first suggesting that the list of statements now known as The Page needed a book to explain them. I am thankful for having Dr. David and Vera Mefford in my life for a number of reasons, but particularly for getting me off my duff about three years ago to actually begin writing. This book would have never reached a coherent stage if it had not been for the excellent editing of another long-time friend, the infinitely patient Roi-Ann Bettez.

Thanks also to those of you who were willing to read early drafts and give me great suggestions for improvement. Eventually we created a readable manuscript. At that point I realized I had no idea how to make it into a book. I started asking anyone who would listen if they knew a publisher and, like magic, The Clark Group appeared. I had heard horror stories about the relationships between authors and publishers. I must say my experience has been just the opposite —The Clark Group has been unfailingly helpful and encouraging. Thanks particularly to Florence Huffman for her attention to the details of line editing and to Bobby Clark for his super-positive encouragement and can-do attitude.

Randy Lisk
February 5, 2008
Lexington, Kentucky

CONTENTS

INTRODUCTION

THE MEETING

I arrived for a routine first meeting with a potential client — an auto parts manufacturer — but it turned out to be not so routine. The client had asked for someone to work with their supervisors to improve what they called people problems. That was to be my job. I am an organizational consultant. My work typically begins as a conversation with an executive who wants help with some mess in his company that is keeping him up at night.

Before I tell you more about that meeting, I'm going to digress briefly to give you a little background of how I got to that time and place. I was born the same year that the transistor was invented. Okay, maybe that is too much digressing, but I wanted to be an engineer before I even knew what an engineer was. I built model planes and electronic gadgets as a kid. In my teen years I graduated to improving the cars I owned — there was always a project of one kind or another underway. I worked my way through college learning how to build and repair electric motors, graduated with a B.S. degree in Electrical Engineering from the University of Cincinnati and was scooped up by IBM.

IBM was kind enough to pay for my master's degree in electrical engineering and give me interesting problems to work on. I was a happy camper. As time went on I held numerous management positions in engineering and planning. I tell my clients that I have already made most of the management mistakes I'm helping them avoid.

In the late 80s IBM, like many other companies, was losing ground in the market place to superior quality products sold at lower prices made by companies with names that we couldn't pronounce. As IBM responded to this competitive threat I got my first exposure to the concepts of quality improvement. This assignment took my problem-solving addiction to a new level. We were talking about company survival and maintaining America's competitive stature in the world. For many of us the problem had been clearly spelled out in NBC's white-paper documentary that aired in 1980: *If Japan Can...Why Can't We?* This documentary introduced America to Dr. W. Edwards Deming as the person credited with jump-starting Japan's manufacturing resurgence after World War II. Deming, an American, was largely unknown in the U.S.

I noticed that many quality problems involved more than electronic circuits and mechanical things. There were these strange variables called employees in the system. (This was a big insight for an engineer). Little did I know that — with this insight — I was about to embark on a whole new journey and learning opportunity!

In 1990 IBM sold our division. I took this occasion to leave IBM and go work with other companies. I've been doing just that ever since. So let's get back to that routine meeting I thought might lead to one more relationship with a new client.

Before the executives signed the contract they wanted to meet me. Our initial contacts had been handled by an intermediary, so I was meeting the executive team for the first time. My plan was to give them an overview of the training and also give them a chance to get to know me.

I would help the supervisors learn to be soft on the people and hard on the problems and to engage the workers to solve more of their own problems. In today's language, I would teach the supervisors to coach. I assumed this meeting was a mere formality and figured the contract was a done deal. The first thing I noticed, as I was escorted into the conference room by the human resources manager, was that he and I were the only non-Asians there. That is not unusual in Kentucky where many fine auto-parts manufacturing companies are Japanese-owned and often Japanese-managed. Most of these executives speak excellent English along with Japanese. At this meeting we had a young lady acting as a translator; she interpreted my comments into Japanese.

I forged ahead and launched into my best explanation of the benefits of coaching. I explained how this method would distribute leadership deeper into the culture and I emphasized how it would increase accountability and commitment. I pointed out how coaching transcends the dilemma of whether to be a hard or a soft supervisor. I received polite nods as each of my sentences were translated. I answered questions about who was the boss and who was the coach. There were more nods and side conversations in Japanese.

What I didn't get was the contract to do the work.

Somewhere in the translation I believe the nuances between coaching and bossing got lost. They decided they did not need my particular expertise. They had enough trouble already.

UNINTENDED CONSEQUENCE: THE PAGE

I hate to lose at anything, even when it is for the best. This meeting felt like a loss and it particularly rankled me because I thought that, at some level, we all wanted the same thing — to improve their results.

As I thought about it more I felt that we did not understand each other when it came to some fundamental beliefs about people and organizations. Not that one of us was right and one was wrong, but I was pretty sure they did not understand where I was coming from. I couldn't be sure of that, because I did not understand most of the conversations, but it was a conclusion that I latched onto to protect my self-esteem. The experience also got me thinking more deeply about what I actually believed about people and organizations. I went home and, in a fit of frustration, wrote down ten statements summarizing what I believed about individuals working in organizations.

The Page was born.

I have modified those ten statements a bit over the years, but nothing of substance has changed. If I have sent you a proposal in the years since that fateful meeting, The Page has been a part of it. My thinking was and is, it is fine if we don't see the world the same way, but I want to make sure anyone who is considering working with me understands up front my thoughts and feelings regarding organizations.

The Page has become my way to begin to build a bridge of understanding for the relationship between me and my clients. It is a statement of my basic beliefs regarding people and organizations. It is my philosophy.

The consultant-client relationship is an interesting one. Like any relationship, it takes time to grow and mature. It is fraught with hopes, fears and expectations on both sides. I have worked with some clients for years. Those relationships are particularly precious to me. These people are more than clients, as our relationship has grown they have become my friends.

On the other hand, sometimes what grows is not what one or both people thought they planted. For example, a number of years ago I did an afternoon of strategic planning with a group of businessmen. The room was hot, people were restless, but when the afternoon was over I thought the group had done a great job of clarifying their desired future. When I checked back with the executive who had hired me, he agreed we got results but he had expected a different result and was underwhelmed by the work. That can happen with best intentions. But thankfully it does not happen often to me.

I now take precautions at the beginning of any work with a new client to get clarity and agreement on the desired results and other variables so that, to the extent possible, what we expect to happen is, in fact, what occurs. The Page is now part of that process.

Would The Page have made any difference with the auto parts company? That is "unknown and unknowable" as Dr. Deming used to say. I'd like to think so.

I have been described to potential clients as an acquired taste so I should not be surprised that the auto parts executives took one taste and moved on down the consultant buffet. A friend of theirs did not say to them "You need Randy Lisk" so I didn't get the benefit of the doubt.

The good news for me is that meeting was the catalyst for The Page. It helped me clarify my own thinking and The Page has become a way for others to get a taste of my ideas about people and organizations.

THE PAGE IS THE BOOK

A long-time friend looked over the ten statements on The Page. He commented that, because he and I had spent so many hours talking about these concepts over the years, he knew what I meant by them — including all the unstated assumptions and connections. But for anyone else, he said, "There is probably a book there." I had to agree.

There is a big difference between meeting a client for the first time and working through a long-term consulting relationship. When clients first read The Page, they often say, "Yes, I understand all these statements. In fact they seem pretty simple."

When the client and I agree to work together, it is much more like a marriage — a mutual commitment to some shared future. And, as in most relationships, the longer you are together, the more deeply you understand each other. I always hope that the amount of disagreement, which is inevitable, stays at a reasonable level as the relationship deepens. After a year of working together the client may look back over those ten simple statements and say, "Now I see what you meant by those statements. I understand them differently now."

One of my reasons for writing this book is to give my clients a way to get that deeper understanding without spending a few years with me.

Another reason for writing this book is the hope that it may influence people to take action to improve both their organizations and their lives. Some of the theory in this book, although not new, will be new to the average manager who is looking for a path to improving his or her craft. My ideas, like most ideas in business books, are built on concepts that have gone before. I have attempted to create this book in a logical way by using some of the basic theories as a foundation. Each person can apply these ideas in new and interesting ways to their organization. Thinking about problems differently is the first step toward improvement.

There can and must be significant improvement in our organizations and society if we are to build a better future. There is an old saying about, "If you want to understand your present circumstances, look to your past behaviors. If you want to understand your future circumstances, look at your present behaviors."

I humbly suggest that the ideas and behaviors suggested in this book, if used, can improve our future circumstances. These new ideas take patience and work, but I have seen them improve people's lives when put into practice.

THE LAYOUT

As you look at the list of ten statements on the next page you will notice they are divided into three parts: individuals, culture and organizations. In this book we will first look at the uniqueness and potential in individuals. Next we'll consider some of the practical aspects of cultural influences such as communication, cooperation and competition. Each chapter will take a deeper look at one of the statements on *The Page*. We'll conclude by exploring the influence of the organizational "S's" such as strategies, systems and structure. The graphic of the concentric ovals illustrates the main ideas of each section of *The Page* and suggests an interrelatedness of all the statements.

THE PAGE

Our work with clients is based on the following assumptions. Everyone does not hold these beliefs. We list them so people we work with will know what to expect from us.

ABOUT INDIVIDUALS:

- Each individual is unique. He or she values ideas, things and people differently and responds to challenges differently. When individuals work together these differences can create chaos or synergy.
- People choose their behavioral responses to what happens to them and are therefore responsible for their own behavior. They choose the best behavior they can think of based on internal and external motivation and their abilities. This behavior may or may not be effective.
- Most people want to do well and succeed. They should have control over how they do their work, and understand why they do their work.
- Leadership resides in every person. It is not reserved just for executives and managers.

ABOUT THE CULTURE:

- A high-trust working environment will create better short and long-term results than a low-trust working environment.
- People need feedback from processes, customers, suppliers and employees of an organization so they can improve. Facts, data and the scientific method provide feedback. Judgment and blame are not feedback.
- An organization is an interdependent system. Competition within a culture creates winners and losers, artificial scarcity and loss. It does not help the organization. Competition between independent organizations is acceptable.

ABOUT ORGANIZATIONS:

- Every organization is perfectly designed to get the results it is getting. The root cause of over 85% of the problems experienced by organizations is found in the systems, strategies, structure, policies, procedures, etc. and NOT directly due to people.
- Organizations and individuals grow and prosper to the extent that they take care of and improve the assets and resources that create the results desired by the stakeholders.
- An organization stays in existence because all stakeholders, including customers, suppliers, employees, owners and the community are willing and able to continue the relationship.

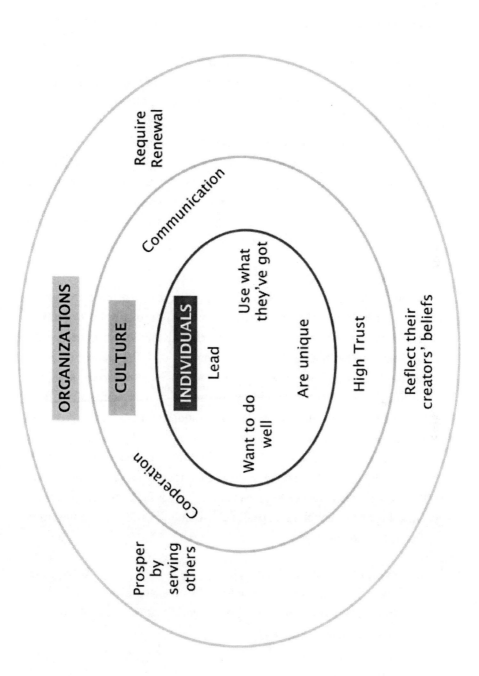

YOUR PAGE

Everyone has a "page" — a list of what he or she believes. Some people have thought about and clarified their beliefs. With others, it is a more nebulous and unexplored topic. If you are involved in any way with an organization as employee, employer, manager, owner, member, officer, team member, board member, or whatever, this book can be an opportunity for you to clarify what you believe about that part of your life.

As you work on your process of clarification, I will give you some of my thinking. Take it as "one way" to see organizations, not "the way" to see organizations. I will encourage you, particularly with a few questions at the end of the chapters, to do the thinking only you can do to clarify your page. If the questions interrupt the flow of the book for you — skip them. In any event I cannot give you your page. That is up to you.

LOOK AT THAT MONSTER

Some of you more mature readers may have had the opportunity to look at a 3-D movie using those colored cardboard glasses — sort of a prehistoric virtual reality. For the rest of you who never had the pleasure, in those bygone days the glasses helped us see the movie in all of its dimensions. The monsters seemed to leap off the screen. Look, it was a long time ago. I'll introduce several pairs of "organizational glasses" or models throughout the book. I am calling them "glasses" because they can help us see organizations more clearly. I agree with the old saying that "All models are wrong. Some are useful." Models are wrong because they are simplifications of reality. They are useful because they give us a way to clarify what is happening. If we go to Mapquest for driving directions, we know the map isn't reality, but it can be helpful getting us where we want to go. I'm going to give you the first pair of glasses now, before we examine any of the statements on The Page.

FOUR LEVELS OF SYSTEM THINKING

In system thinking there is a concept called Four Levels of System Thinking. It is a way of looking at the world that we can apply to organizations. The Four Levels are:

1. Results or Events;
2. Patterns of Behavior Over Time;

3. Structures and Systems; and
4. Beliefs, Assumptions or Mental Models.

The accompanying graphic illustrates the relationship between the Four Levels as an iceberg. Only the top part of an iceberg is readily visible, while the great mass of the iceberg, the more important part, is hidden. The same is true for the Four Levels.

I use the Four Levels to help myself think more deeply and systemically about both personal and organizational problems. For example, suppose I step on the scales and observe that I recently put on unwanted weight. That is a result. In the Four Levels that is a Level 1 result. Going deeper I think about my behaviors over the past few months — Level 2 — including large meals, a little wine in the evening and not much exercise. I think to myself, "How did this happen?"

As I think deeper about the structure of my life — Level 3, structures — I realize I have been on the road a lot, trying to get a lot done and basically putting everything else at the mercy of my work as a good workaholic should, "What was I thinking?" I wonder.

If I am honest and can look at my own beliefs — Level 4 — I may find a fear that if I don't respond to all these opportunities now I may miss out. Reflecting more deeply I see what is happening and now think that perhaps this is not the way I want to lead my life, so I decide to make some structural changes and rebalance life. I believe this will cause a new set of behaviors. With any luck these new behaviors will lead to a lower reading on the scales in the near future and a longer lifetime to take advantage of all those opportunities.

The example about my weight shows how to use the Four Levels to diagnose and prescribe based on a personal issue. This tool can also be used to give us insight into how organizations work. An organization is initially created mentally from the Level 4 beliefs of its founders. The founders used their own mental models of the world and themselves. They relied on these beliefs to create Level 3, the structures and systems of the organization, and populated this creation with people who brought the organization to life with their Level 2 behaviors over time. The Level 1 results of the organization flow from this group behavior.

Beliefs create structures, structures create behaviors, behaviors create results.

The Four Levels graphic reminds us to diagnose problems in organizations by beginning with what is most visible: Level 1 results and work "down" to the largely tacit Level 4 beliefs. This will help us see the deeper causes and not get hooked on the more visible symptoms. When it is time to prescribe or suggest a solution, although changes can be made by working on any of the four levels, we will find that the highest leverage for creating a better future begins by changing Level 4 Beliefs.

The Four Levels model may seem vague and unclear to you right now. Hang in there. Just get a feel for the general idea. We'll be referring back to this model throughout the book to help us give deeper meaning to the statements on The Page. The missing details will fill in for you. If you just can't wait and you must have a more detailed explanation of the Four Levels you can look in *The Fifth Discipline Fieldbook* by Peter Senge et al, beginning on page 97.

Okay, let's grab our glasses and get started.

Four Levels of System Thinking

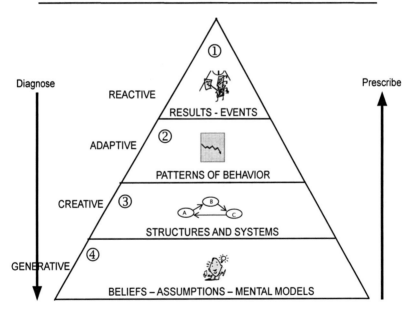

- Level 1. Results or Events are todays headlines – real happenings that we observe – today's crisis
- Level 2. Patterns of Behavior over time are the system's "memory" – actions or variables that have been changing over time
- Level 3. Structures or Systems are the cause and effect relationships between variables, including procedures, laws, policies, rules and hierarchy
- Level 4. Beliefs, Assumptions and Mental Models – the way the world is – internal thinking, tacit assumptions

PART ONE

INDIVIDUALS

THE PAGE

Our work with clients is based on the following assumptions. Everyone does not hold these beliefs. We list them so people we work with will know what to expect from us.

ABOUT INDIVIDUALS:

- *Each individual is unique. He or she values ideas, ~~things~~ and people differently and responds to challenges differently. When individuals ~~work together~~ these differences can create chaos or synergy.*
- People choose their behavioral ~~responses and are~~ therefore responsible for their own beha~~vior. They~~ think of based on internal and external ~~factors that~~ may or may not be effective.
- Most people want to do well and ~~feel good about~~ they do their work, and understand wh~~y and how~~
- Leadership resides in every person. It is not reserved just for executives and managers.

> *Each individual is unique. He or she values ideas, things and people differently and responds to challenges differently. When individuals work together these differences can create chaos or synergy.*

ABOUT THE CULTURE:

- A high-trust working environment will create better short and long-term results than a low-trust working environment.
- People need feedback from processes, customers, suppliers and employees of an organization so they can improve. Facts, data and the scientific method provide feedback. Judgment and blame are not feedback.
- An organization is an interdependent system. Competition within a culture creates winners and losers, artificial scarcity and loss. It does not help the organization. Competition between independent organizations is acceptable.

ABOUT ORGANIZATIONS:

- Every organization is perfectly designed to get the results it is getting. The root cause of over 85% of the problems experienced by organizations is found in the systems, strategies, structure, policies, procedures, etc. and NOT directly due to people.
- Organizations and individuals grow and prosper to the extent that they take care of and improve the assets and resources that create the results desired by the stakeholders.
- An organization stays in existence because all stakeholders, including customers, suppliers, employees, owners and the community are willing and able to continue the relationship.

INDIVIDUALS ARE UNIQUE

CHAPTER 1

THE PAGE

Each individual is unique. He or she values ideas, things and people differently and responds to challenges differently. When individuals work together, these differences can create chaos or synergy.

LOOK AT WHAT?

My wife and I were going somewhere in the car. I was driving.

"Oh man, look at that!" I say.

"What?" she says.

"The car that just went by."

"Which one?"

"Which one?" I ask incredulously,

"The red Ferrari."

"I must have missed it," she says, looking out the window at nothing in particular. Meanwhile, I am wondering how anyone with eyes could miss such a sight.

I love my wife very much and am fortunate that she is in my life. This story shows how we value things differently. It's the kind of story that gets repeated in various guises and themes between most people who spend any amount of time together. It may not be cars. It may be TV shows, or money, or a thousand other subjects. The point is that two people can see the same thing, see it differently and both be right.

I started reading *Hot Rod Magazine* — the pictures were that strange green color — when I was about twelve. By the time I was fourteen I was rebuilding a 1949 Ford in the side yard. I hung out at an old auto body repair shop when I was growing up in Washington Court House, Ohio. It was a one-man operation and the man's name was Morgan Yahn — Morg's Body Shop. I thought that was a cool name. My dad, who is one of my heroes, knew nothing about cars and did not care a whit about them as long as they got him where he wanted to go. My mom took an even dimmer view of my interest, feeling that there must be a recessive gene in me that got out and was running around. All she knew was I had way too much grease under my fingernails. And the fact that I would rather work on a muffler than go to the prom did not help my image with her much.

I honestly don't know where my connection with cars came from and I suppose it doesn't matter. It is a part of who I am. I'm Car People.

My wife drives a nice car. She chooses cars based on safety, looks, handling, highway ride and investment versus payback. That's a great way to do it. I look at cars that way too: I'm all about a good return on an investment. But for me, they should also have a look, a feel, some panache, a certain uniqueness. I can't really explain it. I know it makes no sense to people who do not have pictures of cars in their head.

Because my wife values me and is a nice person, she supports my need to go out and roll in a pile of cool cars every now and then, even though she could care less.

It is inevitable when people get together in a family, on a team, in a business, or as a community, the individuals will value things differently. One person will value other people, seeing them as unique individuals. Someone else may not care that much about other people as individuals but will be concerned about the financial needs of the group.

You can think of examples from the groups you belong to. Having people who value different things and value a given thing differently can be very good for a group because they can complement each other. The different viewpoints create a better chance that the group will be aware of all the critical factors for success and will not undervalue or overvalue one particular factor.

How To Create A World

People believe that they see the world — reality — as it is. Therefore, we think that what we value is the right thing to value. The photograph illustration on the next page may help.

People observe what is happening and filter these observations based on how they understand the world and themselves. These mental filters help create our mental models, what we have called Level 4 in the Four Levels.

These filters cause some portion of what we observe to be overvalued while other parts may be undervalued or ignored. That's why I noticed the Ferrari but my wife didn't — because I like cars more than she.

In addition, people add their own meaning to and make different conclusions about, what they observe. Two people can look at the picture of the young woman and baby in the illustration. One may see a mother's love and the other may see a poorly-cropped picture.

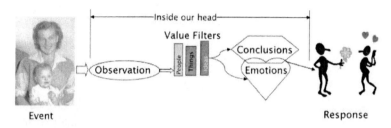

The conclusion creates an emotion in the person, that causes a behavioral response from the person. If I go out to water the back yard, glance down and conclude there is a snake at my feet, I get the heck out of there. Then, maybe I take a second look and it turns out to be the garden hose under a bush. I smile and proceed with the watering. The snake was real to me — in my own three-pound universe between my ears.

Humans either move away from or fight that which appears hurtful. We move toward that which we conclude is good or useful. This is the well-known fight or flight response.

This is a simplified explanation of how we all make our minute-by-minute decisions and try to get our needs met in the world. Humans behave.

Because our individual conclusions cause our decisions, we each see the world as we are rather than as it is. That is, we see the world through our mental filters that bring certain things into clarity while leaving others unclear or unseen. Being human, we only see a partial view of the real world, while someone else sees a different view. That doesn't mean that one of us is right or that the other person is wrong. It just means each person sees his or her own reality.

What is important is how people respond to these different world views. When we attempt to judge, convert, fix, or heal the other person — to show them where they are wrong — we are starting down the road to chaos. When we attempt to understand the scope, significance and possibility in what the other person sees, we are entertaining the possibility of synergy. Synergy requires energy. Chaos happens naturally.

HARTMAN VALUE PROFILE

Humans are a complex mix of different, often conflicting, values, beliefs, passions, talents and wants. Researchers have developed many systems to describe and categorize humans based on different variables. One such system is the Hartman Value Profile. You might consider this our second pair of organizational 3-D glasses, like the Four Levels from chapter 1.

Dr. Robert S. Hartman, born Robert Shirokauer, was a teenager in Hitler's Germany. He observed that Hitler was doing a great job of organizing evil. This led him to ask, *"How do you organize good?"* This question drove his life's work. He was pursued by the Nazis and forced to leave Germany under the new passport name: Robert S. Hartman. He spent the rest of his life researching, consulting and teaching in the US and Mexico. During the course of his life Hartman developed what is now known as the Hartman Value Profile (HVP) as one way to assess how humans value and assign meaning to their external world and themselves. He published *The Structure of Value: Foundations of Scientific Axiology* in 1967.

Axiology literally means the science of value. He is known as the person who combined the rigor of mathematics with the concepts of value. Hartman brought a mathematical formalism called axiology to what had been a subjective area, the study of value. His work earned him a nomination for the Nobel Prize in 1973. Hartman's papers and related documents are housed in the Robert S. Hartman Institute for Formal and Applied Axiology at the University of Tennessee.

Hartman defined three dimensions of value — roughly equivalent to what I have been calling mental filters — for both a person's internal and external world. These three dimensions are: systemic (ideas or mental concepts), extrinsic (things) and intrinsic (people).

To illustrate the three dimensions, when I show people the photograph of the mother and child (page 15) and ask what pops into their head, some say *"two humans,"* or *"a photograph."* Others say, *"One of the people is older than the other,"* or, *"She is a pretty woman."* When asked what they notice, others say, *"A mother's love."* These answers illustrate Hartman's three dimensions.

The world viewed <u>systemically</u> is a black and white, either or world. Everything is evaluated as being a member of a class or group, or not. People who see the picture as two humans or a photograph are seeing it systemically. The systemic is the dimension of mental constructs and ideas. A person who has a clear systemic world view understands rules, systems and hierarchy. A person who views their inner world with a clear systemic view has a solid conceptual view of their future and of their own personal rules of right and wrong.

Concepts can be valued systemically. For example, I am either over six feet tall or under six feet tall. In Iraq, as I write this, whether you are Sunni or Shiite is a systemic distinction that can result in life or death. *"You are either with us or against us"* is a systemic statement.

The world viewed <u>extrinsically</u> is a world of comparisons: a world of categories, of good, better and best; of cause and effect and practical matters. A person who views the picture from the extrinsic perspective might see a poorly cropped picture of one person who is older than the other or a pretty (not ugly) woman wearing an old-fashioned (not modern) dress. People with a clear extrinsic world view are good at practical matters and have a good sense of cause and effect.

Extrinsic skills are useful; for example, think about how you might evaluate different chairs before making a buying decision.

"This one is too hard, this one is too expensive and this one is perfect if they have it in the right color."

This is the language of comparison. It also sounds like the Herman Miller Furniture Company version of *The Three Bears*. There may be a lot of checkpoints on your chair-buying list, but the list is not infinite. You decide what it takes to make a good chair for you and you find a chair that is as close to that list as possible. That is extrinsic valuation.

The <u>intrinsic</u> view of the world sees a world of uniqueness: a world of emotions and potential. A person who views the picture from an intrinsic view sees a mother's love. He sees a happy child with a full life ahead. My intrinsic view of that photograph sees a unique picture of my wife with her mother. In that sense, there is no other photograph like this one. The intrinsic is the richest dimension; we see things through that dimension that are not visible to the naked eye. I could talk forever and not fully capture everything I see in the picture and the people in it.

Intrinsic valuation involves not only thinking about how something looks or feels, but it also involves the feelings generated, or the specialness that sets this one apart from all the others that may be similar. Think about the uniqueness of each human. There are an infinite number of ways to value a human because each is special and unique. We can also value objects intrinsically. If I have a hammer that belonged to my dad and I remember us building things together using the hammer when I was a kid, that hammer is like no other to me. It is special; one of a kind. That is an intrinsic valuation of the hammer.

PEOPLE ARE MORE IMPORTANT THAN THINGS

Hartman concluded that people are more important than things and things more important than concepts. He also concluded that Hitler had reversed the order of importance and that was the basic difference between good and evil.

Some researchers believe it is most useful to have a balanced view of all three dimensions. Individuals who have a clear and balanced view of both themselves and the world around them can see things and circumstances from all three perspectives: systemic, extrinsic and intrinsic. These people tend to have more realistic concepts of what is important, see things others miss, make better decisions and are more sensitive to the needs and concerns of others. They are generally more versatile and objective and are both able and willing to accomplish a wider range of activities.

If a person clearly values both the external world and his or her internal world we say he or she has good soft skills or emotional intelligence.

I have worked with community leaders to identify ways to connect the students in the school system with businesses in our region. We recently heard some research results that listed the following skills as most important for students entering business:

- Able to work with others in teams;

- Able to critically solve problems;

- Able to "learn how to learn"; and

- Able to manage self

These all fall under the category of emotional intelligence.

I have introduced Hartman's Value Profile as one way to describe the uniqueness of people in an organization. Remember the Four Levels glasses from the last chapter? Level 4 consisted of beliefs and mental models. Hartman's Value Profile gives us a way to categorize and define those beliefs. And, as we have seen, Level 4 beliefs applied to an organization eventually create the results. As we better understand how people value themselves and the parts of their world, we can understand how organizations get the results they are getting. The table below summarizes Hartman's categories.

EXTERNAL WORLD	INTERNAL WORLD
Intrinsic — Empathetic Outlook The interpersonal perspective Other people and relationships Feelings and emotions Seeing the potential in others	**Intrinsic — Sense of Self** The "inner-personal" perspective Being — sense of inner worth Knows personal strengths Sees potential of self A person's uniqueness
Extrinsic — Practical Thinking The tangible, observable real world Doing activities Work functions Projects and attention to detail Comparisons of good, better, best	**Extrinsic — Role Awareness** Identifies with key roles, job, family What the individual does Personal satisfaction with roles Balance among key roles Role harmony
Systemic — Systems Judgment Concepts, ideas, mental constructs Thinking activities Laws, policies, rules, procedures Authority Learning, planning	**Systemic — Self Direction** Mental concepts of self Thinking about the future Self organization and discipline Vision of who you will become Personal ethics

Hartman's Value Profile in summary, adapted from *Personal Talent Skills Inventory*™ *Manual*, ©2006 Target Training International Limited and Dr. David and Vera Mefford.

HIDDEN MOTIVATORS

Hartman's approach is one way to understand and describe human uniqueness. Individual uniqueness is an inside job — deeply entrenched in the heart, soul and mind of the individual. People are different because they value different things. Values are the things that people hold as important, such as truth, beauty and love, or science, art and religion.

Values are a necessary part of human life. They are the reason, the why we do things. Steve Morris, an organizational consultant and friend, calls values decision-making priorities.

To help my clients focus on their values I often use a simple assessment based on the work of Eduard Spranger who wrote a book in 1928 entitled *Types of Men*. He identified six major attitudes or values as summarized in the following table:

Theoretical	A passion to discover, systematize and analyze, search for knowledge
Utilitarian	A passion to gain return on investment of time talent and money
Aesthetic	A passion to "be all you can be," to create balance, harmony and beauty
Social	A passion to assist others, particularly those least able to help themselves
Individualistic	A passion to lead, to be in charge and to influence others
Traditional	A passion to live by a defined set of rules and to maintain traditions

DIFFERENT STROKES...

There are many reasons why someone chooses one career over another. A friend of mine swears he became an accountant because the good-looking girl in front of him registered for an accounting class and he decided to attend the same class. (This friend has been known to exaggerate in the past.) We all know people who just seem to be cut out for one career or another. Many times it is because they value what a certain career offers. Let's take a look at how these six values might play out in various careers.

Why would a scientist work tirelessly for ten years trying to discover a new drug? A friend since childhood tells us that this scientist (we'll call her Marie) has always been curious and liked to learn and solve problems. Marie got her first chemistry set for Christmas when she was ten and she first singed her eyebrows with a clean blue flame when she was eleven.

For Marie, solving problems is not something she <u>HAS</u> to do; rather it is something she <u>WANTS</u> to do. Marie's work is in line with her passion. We can be rather certain that this person has a high Theoretical value.

I know engineers and researchers who are always learning about the latest new thing. They are curious problem-solvers. The engineering disciplines provide a constant opportunity for learning and solving problems. People with a high Theoretical value are naturally attracted to this type of work.

<u>Utilitarian</u>

Billy sold the most holiday wrapping paper in junior high school. Now, ten years out of college, Bill is national sales leader for a Fortune 500 company. Bill has always loved to get a return on his investment, whether it is an investment of time, talent, energy, or money. Research has shown that almost three quarters of the top salespeople across a wide variety of industries have Utilitarian as their highest value. Bill is one of these people.

Ask a room full of business people, *"What is the purpose of business?"* A large number will respond, *"To make money for the shareholders."* Their response proves that natural selection of lovers of the bottom line is alive and well in for-profit organizations. These practical, what's in it for me, people have a high Utilitarian value. They drive our capitalist system, particularly if the system is structured so they can reap individual rewards for their own hard work.

Most everyone wants to be paid fairly. The people I am talking about are different. What moves them to action is the thought that they will be well-rewarded for the investment of themselves. Return on Investment (ROI) is one of their measures of success. Put Bill into a challenging sales job and that job becomes intrinsically motivating. Put someone who is not motivated this way into the same job and the odds of success go way down.

Is Bill a good person and the second person a bad person? No. Is Bill better suited, from a motivation point of view, for this particular job than the second person? Yes. Individuals are unique — they respond to situations and challenges differently.

Aesthetic

Consider the starving artist who continues to produce beautiful works of art, even as she worries about how to pay the rent. Creating, being all she can be, the characteristics of a high Aesthetic value, trump the more practical aspects of life. Bill the Utilitarian buys some of her art, but thinks she is weird. You can also find people with a high Aesthetic value employed as strategic planners or system programmers. These people have a knack for envisioning the future or the completed software project before the work starts. These people are not starving.

Social

If Bill the Utilitarian walks through the typical non-profit social service agency and looks at the executive director's job, he is likely to think, *"I would not do this job for this lousy pay."* I know that because I have thought that. When I asked the executive director of the agency why she stayed there, she said, *"This is the best job in the world."* Her Social value, her need to help those who cannot help themselves, was getting met.

Consider this person and others like her in the helping professions: people who are nurses, teachers, social workers and similar professionals. The Social drive — the desire to help those in need, á la Mother Teresa — is strong enough to fill these service positions with people who want to help others, even at a lower salary. This will seem obvious to you if you have a high Social value. Otherwise, you may not understand these people.

Individualistic

There are some people who enjoy being in charge. In high school they were running for senior class president or got elected captain of the cheerleading squad. In later life they became officers in the military and executives in organizations. The common term for this individualistic motivation is 'power.'

The Individualistic characteristic combines with others. For example, I have worked with a number of mayors. A high proportion of them have Individualistic and Social as their top two motivators: be in charge and help others. Many entrepreneurs have Individualistic and Utilitarian as their top two values: be in charge and make money. As I reviewed this topic with one ex-mayor I asked him, *"Were you class president?"*

"All four years," he responded. And then he added, *"But doesn't everybody want to be in charge?"*

His response shows how most of us think that how we see the world is how others see it. We think what we value are the right things to value.

Traditional

I was working with one young lady who had a high Traditional value. When I asked her about it, she told me she had been in the U.S. Army for the last seven years and had adopted the Army's leadership values. Other people with a high Traditional motivation may be very committed to a particular religion, or way of life. People with a high Traditional motivation typically have found a "closed set of rules" for living, such as a religion or an organization's beliefs. Some of these people can become quite narrow-minded with a "my way or the highway" point of view. One terrible example of high Traditional values are the homicide bombers who are willing to lose their life and kill others who violate their beliefs.

There are also many positive examples of people with a high Traditional value who help keep great traditions alive in our communities and help provide a stable foundation for society.

Every job, even suicide bomber, can be motivating for the right person. To discover the motivators in a job, ask the question, *"Why would someone want to do this job? What will he or she get out of it?"* Referring to the six values listed above, some common answers include:

- Learning new things or solving tough problems — theoretical
- Creating results and making money — utilitarian
- Creating something beautiful — aesthetic
- Helping other people or working for a cause — social
- Being in charge or forming alliances — individualistic
- Being a part of something bigger than self — traditional

BE REASONABLE — SEE IT MY WAY

Each of the values has an overextension — a dark side — and it is helpful for all of us to recognize our own tendencies in these areas. The passion becomes the problem. Utilitarians and Workaholics are often found in the same body. The work ethic is so ingrained into our society that workaholism (if that is a word) is one of the few addictions that is generally accepted in this country. Putting too much emphasis on work is a natural "overextension" of the Utilitarian value.

As a person with a high Theoretical value my overextension is paralysis by analysis. That is, I get caught up in the learning and forget why I was supposed to be learning — to create a result.

For example, in the engineering world, sometimes engineers get carried away with researching an interesting part of a project. They often value theory and learning and score high on the Theoretical scale and are plagued by paralysis by analysis.

At this point the Utilitarians in Sales become impatient for practical results. They remind the Theoreticals that it is time to stop learning and create something useful to meet the project deadline. In turn, the Theoretical engineers accuse the Utilitarians of being crass money grubbers who don't understand the finer elements of the technology — whatever the current technology is. The Utilitarians grumble back about the ivory-tower people.

Perhaps all this human uniqueness may not be such a great thing, something most of us notice when someone is taking issue with our opinions. I said earlier that it was useful to have different value viewpoints in a group. But the group must value and appreciate those differences for them to be useful to the group. When individuals work together their differences can create either chaos or synergy.

WE ARE ALL NORMAL — *NOT*

When I worked at IBM the highest organizational reward for a Theoretical person was to be named an IBM Fellow. People who achieved that level were crowned the royal smart people in the land of THINK. They were given carte blanche to study and work on whatever they wanted for five years and were paid well to do so. They were based at Watson Research Center in New York. It was the intellectual freedom that came with that award, not the money per se, that made it special — and motivating — for these people and others who aspired to achieve that position.

When I think about the IBM Fellows I can hear the Utilitarians muttering to themselves, *"Right, intellectual freedom my eye. It was the money that motivated them."* With those words the Utilitarians interpret the achievement in a way that is meaningful to them.

As individuals we all look at the world through our own mental filters. Others who have a similar set of filters see a world like ours. If a person does not value something, such as learning, he will tend to disregard it or even be negative toward it. It is hard for that person to understand how it could be a motivator to someone else. We all tend to self reference our world. We think of ourselves as normal and put ourselves in the middle and then compare others to ourselves.

The result is, if someone values the world differently than we do, we don't describe it as *"Gee, we have different views."* Often we say, or at least think, that we are right and the other person is wrong. In Hartman's scheme, that thought is taking a systemic, or at best an extrinsic view, instead of a more holistic intrinsic view, of the other person. The systemic and extrinsic views do not recognize a person's uniqueness.

Being aware of our passions as well as what we are less interested in is one way for us to begin to understand and value the uniqueness in ourselves and others. In Hartman's terms, we are seeing ourselves and the other person from a more intrinsic point of view.

As we take an intrinsic view of ourselves and others it becomes obvious that we cannot use these six values as ways to pigeonhole or define others. In fact, we should be doing just the opposite since we are all combinations of all six values along with many other variables.

As a simple example, my top two values are Theoretical and Utilitarian. Sometimes these two values disagree about what I should be doing. For instance, I'd like to keep writing on this manuscript right now, but the Utilitarian representative in my head has just pointed out that there are invoices to be sent and work to be done to get prepared for my next client. Sprinkle in the other four values in varying intensities and you can see why it is easy to get a wide variety of views on any subject. Don't make the mistake of simplifying yourself or others.

So What?

People tell me, *"I don't get it. That person is a slug at work. He does as little as possible. He's out the door right at quitting time. But I saw a sign on his van. I didn't know he did house painting. One of my friends used him and said he was great to work with, did a super job and offered a lot of helpful suggestions. I can't believe it."*

Believe it. It happens all the time. The real juice in life comes from intrinsic motivation: the feeling that you <u>want to</u> instead of <u>have to</u>. People who, by whatever means, get their internal motivators lined up with what is required for high performance in their jobs are lucky. They get a shot of this intrinsic motivation every day.

I often help companies align their hiring with the needs of the position. I recently talked with a young person who had just started working in a unique research position. We had, I thought, done a good job of defining the job and searching for the right person to fill it.

"How's it going?" I asked.

"You couldn't pry me out of here," she responded.

There is more to a good job / person match than just the intrinsic motivation piece, but it is certainly one important component.

Those who don't get the kick of internal motivation in their day job try to find some other way to get the fix — through a second job, hobby, volunteer work, or whatever. Or, tragically, they become disconnected from their internal power source (what metaphor do you expect from an old electrical engineer?) and substitute some other lesser source to move them to action. Perhaps they work where they do out of habit, or because they're well paid. Sometimes these people drift toward the land of victims.

"I've got to go to work, don't want to, have to. I hope I win the lottery."

We all have a different mixture of preferences, beliefs, mental filters and assorted craziness at the core of who we are. As we understand how and why we think and feel as we do, it becomes possible for us to consider our thoughts and feelings as only one among many. If there are other possibilities, that means we have choices. Then we can ask ourselves two interesting questions:

1. Is the thought and feeling I habitually use in this situation still the best one?

2. Is it helping me get what I want?

    Asking these questions of ourselves is how we continue to grow and develop.

ORGANIZATIONALLY SPEAKING . . .

You may be thinking, *"Okay, Randy, but what does all this have to do with organizations?"* Good question. Consider that the probability of an organization's success increases as it engages more of its resources in service to its mission. Its competitors are trying to do the same thing.

One resource in every organization is the discretionary energy — the passion — of its people. This particular energy cannot be purchased. It is volunteered, given by choice, at the discretion of its owner. That extra effort seems to be one differentiator between excellent companies and the also-rans. One factor of an organization's success is how well its people match up with the culture and if they are willing and able to employ their talents in service to the mission.

You know the organization is on the right track when people feel they are in a job that was made for them, when they want to come to work, instead of have to and when they work together in cooperative and synergistic ways.

Tip: you can either skip the *Now What?* sections at the end of each chapter or use these questions to help you formulate your own Page.

Now What?

1. Identify your own internal motivators. Match those motivators to the present roles in your life and how you spend your time. How well do they match?

2. Ask yourself, "What do I enjoy doing?" You probably enjoy spending time in the places where there is a match. These are the want to parts of your life.

3. Are there other situations where there is a disconnect or a mismatch? Those are the areas that may be more difficult for you and are probably in your have to category.

4. Identify the motivators in your present job. Are these things that motivate you personally? If not, what does get your motor running? How does this thing that motivates you get played out in your life at this time?

5. Quickly estimate what percent of your life is want to. Don't say, "I don't know." I know you don't know, but if you did know, what would the number be? If that number is lower than you'd like, think of some ways to increase the want to portion of your life. Yes, you can do it.

6. What will your Page say about the uniqueness of humans?

THE PAGE

Our work with clients is based on the following assumptions. Everyone does not hold these beliefs. We list them so people we work with will know what to expect from us.

ABOUT INDIVIDUALS:

- Each individual is unique. He or she values ideas, things and people differently and responds to challenges differently. When individuals work together these differences can create chaos or synergy.

- *People choose their behavioral responses to what happens to them and are therefore responsible for their own behavior. They choose the best behavior they can think of based on internal and external motivation and the abilities. This behavior may or may not be effective.*

- Most people want to do well they do their work, and understand

- Leadership resides in eve s and managers.

> *People choose their behavioral responses to what happens to them and are therefore responsible for their own behavior. They choose the best behavior they can think of based on internal and external motivation and their abilities. This behavior may or may not be effective.*

ABOUT THE CULTURE:

- A high-trust working envi results than a low-trust working e

- People need feedback from processes, customers, suppliers and employees of an organization so they can improve. Facts, data and the scientific method provide feedback. Judgment and blame are not feedback.

- An organization is an interdependent system. Competition within a culture creates winners and losers, artificial scarcity and loss. It does not help the organization. Competition between independent organizations is acceptable.

ABOUT ORGANIZATIONS:

- Every organization is perfectly designed to get the results it is getting. The root cause of over 85% of the problems experienced by organizations is found in the systems, strategies, structure, policies, procedures, etc. and NOT directly due to people.

- Organizations and individuals grow and prosper to the extent that they take care of and improve the assets and resources that create the results desired by the stakeholders.

- An organization stays in existence because all stakeholders, including customers, suppliers, employees, owners and the community are willing and able to continue the relationship.

INDIVIDUAL BEHAVIORAL STYLES

CHAPTER 2

THE PAGE
People choose their behavioral response to what happens to them and are therefore responsible for their own behavior. They choose the best behavior they can think of based on internal and external motivation and their abilities. This behavior may or may not be effective.

I KNOW WHAT YOU ARE THINKING

I was talking with a friend about the differences between observations, assumptions and conclusions. An observation is based on our five senses — externally observable facts and data — and a conclusion is a mental creation.

My friend said, *"I'll give you a great example. Last week I was walking down the hall and a co-worker stopped me and said, 'Why are you mad at me?'*

'Why would you think that?' I asked. 'I'm not mad at you.'

'Yes, you are. You've gone right by my office three or four times in the last week and have not said one thing to me. I can tell you're mad at me. I just don't know why.'"

My friend realized he had been so preoccupied with a project that he probably had gone by the person's office a few times without stopping to check in, as was his usual custom.

There you have it: the perfect set up for a misunderstanding. One of my favorite sayings, attributed to Sam Keen, a noted American author and professor of philosophy and religion, is *"Thought creates the world and then says it didn't do it."*

HOW TO CREATE FICTION

We can use the earlier photo of my wife and her mom on page 15 to explain this interaction. The other person observed my friend's behavior — walking past his office without stopping. Next, that person made up a story that contained assumptions about the observed behavior such as, "This new behavior has something to do with me." The co-worker then drew a conclusion to fit his story — "He is angry with me."

To his credit, the co-worker talked to my friend about what he had observed. By checking out his conclusion, the co-worker eliminated an erroneous thought that would have undoubtedly "festered into fact," as Mr. Keating says in the movie, *The Dead Poets' Society*.

Many times these fictional mental stories do not get checked out. The person who concocts the story treats it as fact instead of only one of many possibilities. In this situation, if that conclusion does not get checked out, the co-worker — assuming that my friend was angry with him — might begin to react. For instance, he could avoid my friend. Sooner or later my friend would notice this behavior and could conclude that, for some reason, the co-worker was angry with him. The general structure of this two-person misunderstanding dance is shown in the following graphic. You can start anywhere and follow the arrows.

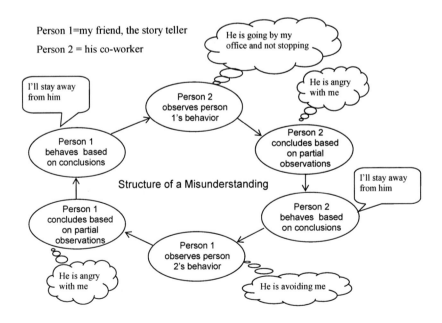

BEHAVIOR — THE RESPONSE TO OUR STORY

In the preceding chapter we said that people value different things and make decisions based on these values. Each of us pays more attention to some things than others. We judge things that happen as good or bad. Our internal filters influence how we see and describe both our inner world and the external world around us. We want the partial reality we observe through these filters to make sense from our point of view, so we piece together a story to fit our filtered observations.

Based on this flawed assessment, we choose some thought, feeling and action as our response — our behavior. Because it is always based on partial data, the behavior we choose may or may not be effective.

Much of my work involves helping people create other possibilities by looking at their observations and conclusions in a different way; in essence, telling a better story. When a person sees a situation differently, his behavior changes. People's results, for better or worse, come from behavior. As Ron Ernst, a friend and executive coach says, *"You can't think or feel your way to a result. You must DO something."* The doing is the key part of behavior. We choose to do something thousands of times a day, to meet some need. From getting up when the alarm goes off until we hit the pillow at night, humans behave. We are as much human doings as human beings.

Our behavior is used by others as the data that they observe and process to make sense out of what is happening. Our behavior is the starting point for the story the other person tells. In that sense, our behavior has a lot to do with how others respond to us. Some behaviors are effective in that they help us get what we want. Other behaviors have the opposite effect. To make matters worse, we are often unaware of the impact of our behavior on others.

PATTERNS OF BEHAVIOR

There are all kinds of sayings about *"It is not what happens to you. It is your response to what happens to you that creates your life."* Something happens to you. You observe what happened, evaluate it and choose a behavioral response. This all happens quickly and it does not always feel like a choice. Over time, these quick, semi-conscious choices become patterns — habits.

IT'S NOT MY FAULT

When we describe to others what is happening to us and our response — when we tell others our story based on our beliefs, assumptions and partial data — we may use language that reflects a seeming lack of choice. We say and hear it every day, *"I had to do that." "She made me so mad." "I can't talk to her about that issue."*

When a person says or thinks, *"I don't have a choice,"* the implied assumption is, "I can't choose a different response." This way of thinking can become victim mentality. If it becomes a habit it leads to: *"I am stuck. I cannot create a different future around this issue."* The victim says, in effect, *"I don't like what is happening to me and I can't do anything about it."*

I believe we choose our behavior. The victim's story, which may be true, is only one of many stories that could be told around the same circumstances. Remember from the Four Levels that Level 2 behaviors create Level 1 results. If we do not choose our behaviors, our future is in someone else's hands, with us playing no part. This is just not true most of the time and is a limiting belief if a person indeed wants to create a different future.

Each of us has natural behavioral responses that we use over and over. We have carried most of our basic responses with us since youth. Think about a time when you have bumped into some old friends from high school, people you have not seen for a while. (I'm assuming you have been out of high school for awhile, although you still look really young). You notice certain things these people do and you remember they did those same things in high school. Those old responses have served them well, so they've hung on to them. Over time these responses have become automatic. Most of us don't even know we are using them.

Behaviors are like mutual funds: past success does not guarantee future success. Conditions change and the responses we used in the past may or may not be effective in the present.

PEOPLE WATCHING, IN THE MIRROR

The first step to understanding this phenomenon is to begin to observe your self and others. Recognize your current responses. Each person is unique. And yet, there are a few simple classifications of behavioral styles that can help categorize different behavioral choices.

Are you more of an introvert or more of an extrovert? Do you prefer working with things or people? Do you have a short temper or rarely get angry?

Are you a rule-follower or a rule-breaker? Are you a poker-face or do you wear your heart on your sleeve?

DISC SURVEY

Another way to understand behavioral styles is to use an empirical tool. Most people have heard of the Myers-Briggs behavioral assessment. It categorizes people into one of sixteen types. If you are at a cocktail party, you are almost as likely to hear something like, *"I'm an ENTJ, what about you?"* as you would *"I'm a Gemini. What's your sign?"* Myers-Briggs provides a rough cut at behavior. Most people fall somewhere between one of the 16 categories and are a combination of several types. Over the years, researchers have built on and improved the basic Myers-Briggs assessment.

I use a well-documented and validated version of a behavioral assessment that provides over 350 different classifications of behavior. Not surprisingly, it provides a more accurate assessment than Myers-Briggs about how a person prefers to get his or her needs met in the world, how the person prefers to be communicated with and managed and what emotions may most likely be felt by this person. The survey is a relatively accurate measure of behavior and is easy to administer. It is like an expert people watcher. Behavior is essentially the language of the people watcher.

This assessment measures four factors: Dominance, Influence, Steadiness and Compliance. We often refer to it as a DISC survey.

The four factors taken together, like the slide switches on an audio system, make up the unique behavioral style of the person. On a home theatre system, slide the switch up, increase the bass. In this system, slide the D switch up, get a little more dominance. People's slide switches can be anywhere from all the way to the bottom, to somewhere in the middle, to all the way to the top. Behavioral uniqueness comes from all the possible combinations of these four variables.

These factors are easy to learn if you spend a little time with them and most people can get rather good at typing another person just by observing that person's behavior. We are often better at typing others' behavior than recognizing our own. Many of us experience blind spots — and not just in our rear-view mirrors.

From looking at a person's DISC graph, we can gain a lot of information about that person's behavior, how she prefers to be communicated with, her preference in jobs, how she will fit on the team and many other useful behavioral-based traits. A person's DISC profile can be shown graphically as in the following:

<hr/>

Four Basic Dimensions of Behavioral Style

Dominance	Influence	Steadiness	Compliance
extroverted	extroverted	introverted	introverted
quick to anger	optimistic, trusting	non-emotional	fears criticism
impatient, direct	"Sells" others	"1-ball juggler"	rule-follower

introverted	introverted	extroverted	extroverted
slow to anger	pessimistic	emotional	independent
patient, indirect	distrusting	"7-ball juggler"	rule breaker
	"tells" others		

HIRE THE SQUIRREL

This graphic helps us think about what behaviors a particular job requires for excellent results. Notice the slide switches. The D and I are above the midline and the S and C are below the midline.

Now think about a typical outside sales job. You would probably agree that this position requires a competitive, action-oriented person. In our behavior language we would say that job needs a person with above-average Dominance (Hi D) in her preferred behavioral style. This job succeeds by selling to the buyer; influencing with words, social interaction and optimism (Hi I). The sales job requires flexibility and a sense of urgency and the ability to keep a number of projects going at once (Low S). Finally the out-bound sales job requires an independence to do what it takes to get the results (Low C). This graphic shows the kind of behavioral style we want to hire for sales.

People whose natural behavioral style falls into these persuader and promoter categories are typically better suited for the demands of this sales job from a behavioral point of view. In simple terms, their natural behavior is the behavior required for superior performance in this job. They will tend to move to opportunities quicker and experience less job stress than someone who has a different behavioral style.

As we discussed in previous chapters, the notice on the side of this carton says: WARNING — success in any position depends on many factors including behavioral style, talent, motivation, hard skills, experience and desire, among others. The kind of behavioral style match that we have been discussing does not, by itself, guarantee success in a job. In fact, we suggest using a number of assessments to match positions to job candidates. However, a behavioral match is certainly one important aspect of achieving a great fit between person and position.

Having said that, the reverse is also true. That is, put someone who is not well-suited from a behavioral standpoint into a job and they most certainly will have more trouble succeeding, as they attempt to modify their natural behavior to fit the job.

My own behavioral style is summarized on the DISC graphic below.

My D and I are low; well below the mid-line. My S and C are well above the mid-line. I am a patient and persistent person who sometimes has trouble getting started on things. Once I get started I keep at it until it is done and done right. Don't bother me with anything else while I am working on the one thing.

Could I be a sales person? Yes. Would it require me to adapt my behavior — to be a different person, behaviorally? Absolutely. Over time, would this take a toll on me, my enthusiasm, my level of stress and burnout? Yes.

Randy's Behavioral Style

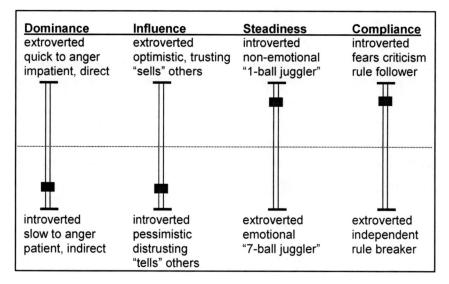

Dominance	Influence	Steadiness	Compliance
extroverted	extroverted	introverted	introverted
quick to anger	optimistic, trusting	non-emotional	fears criticism
impatient, direct	"sells" others	"1-ball juggler"	rule follower
introverted	introverted	extroverted	extroverted
slow to anger	pessimistic	emotional	independent
patient, indirect	distrusting	"7-ball juggler"	rule breaker
	"tells" others		

Or, put another way, you can teach a turkey to climb trees, but it is easier to hire a squirrel.

YOU'RE PERFECT, NOW CHANGE

Different jobs require different behaviors to do them effectively. I'll bet you know a successful salesperson (or engineer) who got promoted to manager and either did not do a great job, or, did not enjoy the job. Why would we think a successful sales person would be a successful sales manager?

Let's look closer at our successful sales person who gets promoted to sales manager. In her new job "winning" means to make or exceed the sales quota assigned to her and her team. Winning is important to a competitive High D person. Only now she must depend on people who work for her, rather than just on her own actions. As it gets close to the end of the quarter and her numbers are not what they should be, what could be more normal than to use her behaviors that have worked before? Be aggressive; take action, "Get It Done!" Only now this behavior that was effective before is seen by those who report to her as blunt, pushy and bordering on downright nasty. When she receives feedback that says these behaviors are less than sterling management qualities, she is blindsided. *"What? Me pushy?"* she says. *"This behavior has always worked before. My manager is an idiot."*

SO WHAT?

The first step to more effective behavior is to have a clear picture of your present behavioral style — your actions, including blind spots. The next step is realizing that, although our natural or preferred behavioral style is relatively hard-wired into us, we can still choose to adapt or choose a different behavior for a given situation. Most of us do some of that every day. Adapting, while extremely useful for certain situations, does require more energy than your natural style. That is why you want to spend the majority of your time behaving in a natural way and not playing a role. As you learn to notice your behavior and modify it to respond more effectively to situations, you have become less the victim of your past and more the creator of your future.

NOW WHAT?

Think about your current job and other major life roles.

1. Are you able to use your natural behavioral style or do these roles require you to be a different person? Do you put on a behavioral mask when you get dressed for work or in any of your other roles?

2. What about your next job?

3. What can you do to make sure it will be a good behavioral fit with your natural style?

4. Behavior is one of several important factors that determine how well a person matches up to the requirements of a particular job and organization. Behavior is a key factor in job success and enjoyment — it should be considered carefully when changing jobs or other roles.

5. If you are having trouble dealing with another person, is it possible the behavior you find annoying is the best behavior that person can come up with, even if it is not effective? Is it possible the other person does not realize what a negative impact their behavior is having on you? Can you do anything about it or do you see yourself as a victim of circumstances?

6. What would your Page say about human behavior — yours and others?

THE PAGE

Our work with clients is based on the following assumptions. Everyone does not hold these beliefs. We list them so people we work with will know what to expect from us.

ABOUT INDIVIDUALS:

- Each individual is unique. He or she values ideas, things and people differently and responds to challenges differently. When individuals work together these differences can create chaos or synergy.
- People choose their behavioral responses to what happens to them and are therefore responsible for their own behavior. They choose the best behavior they can think of based on internal and external motivation and their abilities. This behavior may or may not be effective.
- *Most people want to do well and succeed. They should have control over how they do their work, and understand why they do their work.*
- Leadership resides in every person. It is not re[serve]d just for executives and managers.

ABOUT THE CULTURE:

- A high-trust working enviro[nment produces better] results than a low-trust working env[ironment].
- People need feedback from [...] [employ]ees of an organization so they can improve. Facts, data and the scientific method provide feedback. Judgment and blame are not feedback.
- An organization is an interdependent system. Competition within a culture creates winners and losers, artificial scarcity and loss. It does not help the organization. Competition between independent organizations is acceptable.

ABOUT ORGANIZATIONS:

- Every organization is perfectly designed to get the results it is getting. The root cause of over 85% of the problems experienced by organizations is found in the systems, strategies, structure, policies, procedures, etc. and NOT directly due to people.
- Organizations and individuals grow and prosper to the extent that they take care of and improve the assets and resources that create the results desired by the stakeholders.
- An organization stays in existence because all stakeholders, including customers, suppliers, employees, owners and the community are willing and able to continue the relationship.

Most people want to do well and succeed. They should have control over how they do their work, and understand why they do their work.

INDIVIDUALS WANT TO DO WELL

CHAPTER 3

THE PAGE

Most people want to do well and succeed. They should have control over how they do their work, and understand why they do their work.

HIRED HANDS

I was asked to be the after-dinner speaker for a professional group. The title of my talk was "We Hired Workers But Human Beings Showed Up." My dad called that "kidding on the square," meaning using humor to deal with a serious subject. During the meal a gentleman at my table said, *"Where I work we hire 'em from the neck down."*

It was difficult for me to respond, even if my mouth hadn't been full of salad. In his company they literally were not hiring human beings.

Fully-equipped human beings come with hands and backs, but also heads, hearts and souls as standard equipment. They also come equipped with a variety of talents. Whether the organization taps into these intrinsic riches is optional and reflects its beliefs about the roles of managers and workers.

I grew up in south central Ohio — farm country — where I first heard the phrase hired hands. In this hi-tech age where brainpower is a competitive advantage it is hard to imagine a company hiring a human being and only using the hands. For people to succeed in organizations and, therefore, for organizations to succeed, everyone needs to use all their parts above and below the neck. The common jargon for this today includes involved and engaged employees.

I believe that most people want to do well and succeed. I explicitly state that on *The Page* because I'm not sure many organizations share this belief. When I hear remarks like the gentleman at dinner made, it makes me wonder. My belief certainly was not shared in his organization.

XTRINSIC MOTIVATION

The "hiring from the neck down" comment told me a lot about how that company manages people and how their managers view the people with whom they work.

Put on your Four Levels glasses and recall that Level 4 beliefs produce Level 3 structures. What kind of work place can you see structurally evolving from a belief like "We hire 'em from the neck down?" I see a place of high control where *"If I want your opinion, I'll give it to you."* I also see a place of high turnover due to hiring from the neck down, as we discussed in the previous chapter. I am sure you can see similar characteristics. Certainly valuing employees from the neck down is not valuing them intrinsically as unique human beings.

This company is not alone in their beliefs. Douglas McGregor wrote a book published in 1960 called *The Human Side of Enterprise*. In the book he defined two ways to think about managing people, which he labeled Theory X and Theory Y.

THEORY X AND THEORY Y

Theory X and Theory Y can be another pair of organizational glasses. In McGregor's day, the late 50s, he believed Theory X was the predominant approach used by organizations. He said, *"The human side of economic enterprise today is fashioned from propositions and beliefs such as these. Conventional organization structures, managerial policies, practices and programs reflect these assumptions."*

McGregor was ahead of his time. He said that these beliefs resulted in structures in organizations. Or, using our Four Levels language, Level 4 beliefs create Level 3 structures.

If you look at the following table, you will notice that McGregor's first point is the same for both theories. He believed that people who held either theory would agree on the role of management: to organize elements in the interest of the organization.

McGregor's Two Assumptions About Managing People

Theory X	Theory Y
1. Management is responsible for organizing the elements of productive enterprise – money, material, equipment, people – in the interest of economic ends.	1. Management is responsible for organizing the elements of productive enterprise – money, material, equipment, people – in the interest of economic ends.
2. With respect to people, this is a process of directing their efforts, motivating them, controlling their actions, modifying their behavior to fit the needs of the organization.	2. People are not by nature passive or resistant to organizational needs. They have become so as a result of experience in organizations.
3. Without the active intervention of management, people would be passive, even resistant, to organizational needs. They therefore must be persuaded, rewarded, punished, controlled – their activities must be directed. This is management's task in managing subordinate managers or workers.	3. The motivation, the potential for development, the capacity for assuming responsibility, the readiness to direct behavior towards organizational goals are all present in people. Management does not put them there. It is the responsibility of management to make it possible for people to recognize and develop these human characteristics for themselves.

CONTROL AND / OR FREEDOM

Reread theories X and Y, comparing points 2 and 3. The differences between the two theories lie in the beliefs about HOW to accomplish the management role.

People in organizations who believe the Theory X set of assumptions use management approaches from hard (coercion, fear) to soft (be nice, warm and fuzzy) and the combination of firm but fair (walk softly and carry a big stick.) All these approaches are variations on the same theme — management by control.

What belief creates a fifteen-step procedure that a worker must follow to get a manager's approval before attending a funeral? Perhaps one that says workers cannot be trusted and must be controlled by rules. What belief causes a person to say, *"We hire 'em from the neck down?"* It might be the belief that managers must control workers because workers cannot, or will not, think for themselves in service to the organization and its goals.

McGregor believed that management by control — whether it be hard, soft or in-between — would ultimately fail because, as Abraham Maslow had already pointed out, control is a useless method to motivate people whose psychological and safety needs are already reasonably met. This insight led McGregor to develop Theory Y.

McGregor believed that Theory Y was the task of managers: *"The essential task of management is to arrange organizational conditions and methods of operation so that people can achieve their own goals best by directing their own efforts toward organizational objectives."* He goes on to say, *"This is a process primarily of creating opportunities, releasing potential, removing obstacles, encouraging growth and providing guidance."*

Can you see the difference? Theory X places exclusive reliance on external control of human behavior, whereas Theory Y relies heavily on intrinsic self-control and self-direction, enabled by a supportive working environment created by managers.

The choice to rely primarily on intrinsic or extrinsic sources of motivation stems from deeper beliefs about the motivations of workers in organizations. Different Level 4 beliefs (Theory X or Theory Y) create different Level 3 structures (high control or high freedom) that create different Level 1 results.

Peter Scholtes is a well-known consultant who has contributed to our knowledge about organizations, particularly in the area of doing away with appraisals. A client once said to him, *"The problem is we have all this dead wood in our organization."* Peter asked, *"Why did you hire dead wood?" "We didn't hire dead wood"* was the reply. *"Well,"* said Peter, *"Then what did you do to kill it?"*

Creating the working environment, whether supportive or toxic, is the job of management. A working environment with too much control will kill the innate enthusiasm and intrinsic commitment that people can bring to their work. That is how to create dead wood, in case you ever need to.

Theory Y managers create environments that nurture growth rather than kill it.

IBM: I've Been Motivated

When I first went to IBM's management school at Dellwood Country Club in upstate New York in the mid-70s, the first thing I learned was that the key duties for a manager were to plan, organize and control. That was enlightened Theory X management. Then they looked at my somewhat overweight pudgy body and added, *"And if you can't control yourself, how will you control others? See you in the morning for pre-breakfast exercise."* Arrgh.

As I work with today's managers, the sons and daughters of the people I exercised with, I emphasize that managers' duties are to coach, help, remove roadblocks and try not to get in the way. Those are two very different sets of assumptions about management.

Who Is In Charge Here?

When I talk to my clients about a Theory Y type of managing I often get some pushback. I'm not surprised. In many cases making that change requires a major shift in both thinking and doing.

I've heard all the objections to Theory Y including *"the inmates are running the asylum"* and a *"country-club atmosphere."* I've also sensed the unspoken fears of managers who know the X game very well and are not particularly interested in learning the Y game. *"If a manager can't tell people what to do, what good is he?"* they ask. Or the ever popular, *"That soft stuff might work in some industries, but not ours."*

As we begin to think deeply about these two assumptions, X and Y, we come across an apparent paradox, sometimes stated as freedom through control. An interesting question is, *"How can managers organize the work and the workers, as McGregor said was their task for both X and Y theories and create environments that nurture growth, without controlling the work?"* How can control, the restriction of freedom, lead to freedom? How can we achieve quality — often defined as reducing variation — by allowing variation?

Organizations are complex living systems and change is the nature of every living system. No system can survive for long without the flexibility to adapt to the changing demands of the outside world. Too much control with too little freedom to change creates a dead system. Look at any deregulated industry such as the telephone or electric power industries. See how the rules have changed with deregulation. Notice who is still around and who is not. Adapt or die.

On the other hand, too much freedom without enough control leads to chaos, anarchy, or, at the very least, a lot of variation. There is an old joke that summarizes the problem of freedom without control: *"We tried to start an anarchist community but no one would obey the rules."* In the 70s at IBM we said, *"IBM loves wild ducks, as long as they fly in formation."*

Balancing freedom and control is an area of management mastery. Those who do it well have a mature understanding of both sides of the paradox. That, to me, is Theory Y management. It is not easy. If you look back over a few organizations' history you will notice that a predominately high-control CEO will often follow a high-release CEO and vice-versa.

I'M A SUPERVISOR. I HAVE SUPER-VISION.

Workers cannot do what McGregor recommends unless they understand why they are doing the work and understand *how* to do the work. Tim Gallwey, author of *The Inner Game of Work*, uses the equation $P = p\text{-}I$ or Performance equals potential minus interference. The potential is inherent in people. Management's job is to remove the interference while creating environments that nurture growth.

I have heard managers say, *"I told her what to do but she just didn't do it."* My glib retort is, *"I guess she just wanted to disappoint you."*

It is easy for Theory X managers to blame the person doing the work for poor results. They have a belief to support their disappointment: point 3 under Theory X. As an added bonus, this belief shows that failure is not the Theory X manager's fault. People are just basically lazy or incompetent — and Theory X proves it.

Judgment and the accompanying blame are as much a part of us as reality shows on television and about as useless. My smart-alec comment above was judgment. "The worker screwed up again" is a judgment. Although management involves evaluating conditions and making decisions based on best information, judgment may not be the best way to create an environment that nurtures growth.

Judgment is quick, decisive, black and white, systemic and efficient. When we judge, we believe we know "the truth, the whole truth and nothing but the truth." Unfortunately, that condition almost never occurs. Creating an environment that nurtures growth is slow, subjective, shaded with gray, intrinsic and effective. As noted in Chapter 2, our truth may not be *the* truth.

If we could rewind the tape we may find that the employee doing the work was:

- Not properly instructed how to accomplish the process
- Did not understand what the finished product should look like
- Did not know how the finished product or service would be used
- Did not receive the assistance and support from others who were involved
- Was never taught how to effectively get assistance from others
- Does not particularly like to do the job
- Was not motivated, extrinsically or intrinsically, to do excellent work on this task
- (You may add other reasons from your own experiences)

To help people understand the what and why of their work, the Theory Y manager needs a complete process for teaching others how to do their work and why they are doing the work.

Telling them, while necessary, is hardly ever sufficient. I recommend that the manager or trainer go through any procedure several times, stressing different aspects each time. This is a great opportunity to use the balance of freedom and control to teach someone. For example:

1. Go through the procedure, focusing on the various process steps. Tell the learner WHAT to do at each step. Explain what the desired result should look like, along with how long it may take to complete the procedure (control).

2. Go through the procedure again. This time focus specifically on HOW to do each step. Make sure the learner has a working knowledge of any

tools, software, skills, etc. needed to complete the procedure. Point out any tips or roadblocks you may know about. Show the learner where he or she can get into trouble. Show the learner where he or she can go to get help if needed (freedom).

3. Go through the procedure a third time, this time explaining WHY the procedure is now being done this way. It should sound something like, *"We believe this is the best way to complete this procedure today. Therefore you need to follow this process. (control) As you become more familiar with the procedure I expect you to come up with some improvements to this procedure. (freedom). When we all agree your ideas for improvement are a better way to do it, we will incorporate them into the process immediately." (freedom)*

4. Ask the learner to perform the procedure. Observe and provide support. If the learner is not performing the procedure correctly, determine if your training needs improvement.

5. Together with the learner, identify measures such as speed, quality, cost, turn-around time or other benchmarks that the learner and you can use as objective measures of performance. (Control by measurements; freedom in joint decisions).

TWO ASSUMPTIONS ABOUT PEOPLE

THEORY X	THEORY Y
1. Management is responsible for organizing the elements of productive enterprise—money, material, equipment, people—in the interest of economic ends.	1. Management is responsible for organizing the elements of productive enterprise—money, material, equipment, people—in the interest of economic ends.
2. With respect to people, this is a process of directing their efforts, motivating them, controlling their actions, modifying their behavior, to fit the needs of the organization.	2. People are NOT by nature passive or resistant to organizational needs. They have become so as a result or experience in organizations.
3. Without active intervention of management, people would be passive, even resistant, to organizational needs. They therefore must be persuaded, rewarded, punished, controlled—their activities must be directed. This is managements' task in managing subordinate managers or workers.	3. The motivation, the potential for development, the capacity for assuming responsibility, the readiness to direct behavior towards organizational goals are all present in people. Management does not put them there. It is the responsibility of management to make it possible for people to recognize and develop these human characteristics for themselves.

Plan, organize and control	Coach, help and facilitate Performance = potential—interference

CONTROL	FREEDOM
Rules	Creativity
Standardization	Innovation
Quality	Improvement
Systemic	Intrinsic

THERE IS NO TIME FOR THIS

Yes, I know each manager doesn't have time to teach every process to her many workers. How much time do you have for fighting fires, attending meetings about quality problems, overseeing an expedited redo of something or, worse yet, listening to a customer bend your ear about a defective product they are holding in their hand?

Make a little time to start this work yourself, or have someone else do it and you check on the training and results. As I said earlier, I get pushback because this work requires managers to think and act differently.

If you agree that workers need to know what they are expected to do and why they are doing it, then your challenge becomes how to develop systems to pass on this knowledge, without doing it all yourself. I'm sure several ideas come to your mind quickly and even more will pop up if you ask the people you work with. Perhaps the new hire orientation process needs improvement. Perhaps a mentor / protégé relationship needs to be established with new hires. Perhaps processes need to be written and proficiency exams passed as a part of the new-hire training.

Perhaps you can't do all of these things personally. And, they won't all be in place tomorrow. What you can do is envision the work, get it started, encourage it and help remove roadblocks and, in general, find ways to create an environment that nurtures growth.

Putting out fires and being a crisis manager, while perhaps necessary at times, is not creating an environment that nurtures growth. Or, as Dr. Deming said, *"If your kitchen catches on fire and you put out the fire, you have not improved your house."* When this growth that you are nurturing occurs, your work life will get simpler and you will have more time for (you guessed it) creating an environment that nurtures growth.

JOYFUL WORK

Someone once asked Dr. Deming how he would summarize what his work was about. He initially responded that his work was about the application of statistics to organizations. Then, after reflecting for a moment, he said his work was about *"bringing joy to work."*

At its best, that should be what all of our work is about. Joy is an intrinsic motivation. It is a human's choice and right to be joyful. It is hard to feel joyful about your work if you are not at least partially in control of what you do. And, it is hard to feel joy if you do not know the purpose of your work — why you are doing it. Unfortunately, for many people, joyful work is as much an oxymoron as jumbo shrimp.

Theory Y assumes that the people who do the work are capable of and responsible for improving the work process. After all, they are the ones who know the most about it. Of course, if they do not know how to do the work or do not know why the work is being done, there is little chance that they will improve the work.

A feeling of ownership and pride of accomplishment are two of the benefits of intrinsic motivation and involvement. This only happens when complete human beings — those with heads, hearts, hands, backs and souls — are involved with what they are doing. It will not happen with hired hands.

"Y" BOTHER?

What is the big deal with Theory Y? Why not just tell the workers what to do and get on with it instead of wasting time with all this soft nice stuff?

The Gallup Organization, a large consulting and research firm, uses a number of questions to assess how engaged a group of employees may be. They contend that higher engagement scores correlate with a better bottom line, higher customer satisfaction and retention, higher morale, lower turnover, etc.

There is plenty of evidence that this soft approach with people leads to better hard returns for the shareholders, workers and others involved with the organization.

Dr. Deming, talking about winning and losing, said there are only two states: win-win or lose-lose. The other two states of win-lose and lose-win are temporary. You can run a win-lose sweat shop for awhile, until the people sweating find other options, or you can run a lose-win laissez-faire country club for a while, until you need to get results. Either approach goes to lose-lose in the long run.

Treating people as if they are more than hired hands and involving them in their work is not soft. In their classic book *Getting To Yes*, Fisher and Ury say *be soft on the people and hard on the problem.* That is a good approach. There is a balance point between the sweat shop and the country club and it is found when you use Theory Y assumptions.

NOW WHAT?

McGregor, referring to Theory X, stated five more additional beliefs which he said were less explicit but widespread in the late 50s. I will paraphrase them slightly.

- The average person is lazy and works as little as possible.
- The average person lacks ambition, dislikes responsibility and prefers to be led.
- The average person is inherently self-centered and indifferent to organizational needs.
- The average person is, by nature, resistant to change.
- The average person is not very bright, *"the ready dupe of the charlatan and the demagogue."*

1. Look over that list of assumptions and on a scale of 0-10, rate how much it appears that your present organization was built on those beliefs. 0 = not at all, 10 = X Inc.

2. What could you choose to do, in your part of the organization, to create a more Y-like organization?

3. On a scale of 0-10, 0=sweat shop, 10=country club, where would you rank your organization? If the number is not optimum for you, what can you do to move the number in the right direction?

4. What are your personal beliefs with respect to the above list? If your numbers are higher than you would like, consider whether or not these assumptions will help you and your organization achieve better results.

5. What would your Page say about the motivation of people?

THE PAGE

Our work with clients is based on the following assumptions. Everyone does not hold these beliefs. We list them so people we work with will know what to expect from us.

ABOUT INDIVIDUALS:

- Each individual is unique. He or she values ideas, things and people differently and responds to challenges differently. When individuals work together these differences can create chaos or synergy.
- People choose their behavioral responses to what happens to them and are therefore responsible for their own behavior. They choose the best behavior they can think of based on internal and external motivation and their abilities. This behavior may or may not be effective.
- Most people want to do well and succeed. They should have control over how they do their work, and understand why they do their work.
- *Leadership resides in every person. It is not reserved just for executives and managers.*

ABOUT THE CULTURE:

- A high-trust working environment will create bette[r] [   ] [a]nd long-term results than a low-trust working envir[onment.]
- People need feedback from p[r   ] [   ] [employe]es of an organization so they can imp[rove   ] [   ] [an]d provide feedback. Judgment and blame[   ]

Leadership resides in every person. It is not reserved just for executives and managers.

- An organization is an interdependent system. Competition within a culture creates winners and losers, artificial scarcity and loss. It does not help the organization. Competition between independent organizations is acceptable.

ABOUT ORGANIZATIONS:

- Every organization is perfectly designed to get the results it is getting. The root cause of over 85% of the problems experienced by organizations is found in the systems, strategies, structure, policies, procedures, etc. and NOT directly due to people.
- Organizations and individuals grow and prosper to the extent that they take care of and improve the assets and resources that create the results desired by the stakeholders.
- An organization stays in existence because all stakeholders, including customers, suppliers, employees, owners and the community are willing and able to continue the relationship.

LEADERSHIP

CHAPTER 4

THE PAGE

Leadership resides in every person. It is not reserved just for executives and managers.

A SIMPLE QUESTION

I was at a meeting at church. We were talking about how to involve more people in running the church. Our idea was to diffuse the leadership into the congregation where appropriate to free up more of the rector's time. We were looking for ways to develop the leadership skills and abilities of more people so they would be comfortable and effective running committees, or doing whatever else they wanted to help the parish. Our principle was "no involvement, no commitment."

This idea of diffused leadership was not roundly applauded by everybody. There are always people who want the leader (rector) to be the general on the white horse, calling the shots and taking the heat. They think we should put the rest of the congregation in pews, where they belong. One of these people said to me, in what felt like a challenging tone, *"What do you think leadership is, anyway?"*

That may sound like a simple question, but if you have looked in a bookstore lately, or Googled the term, you found a google of references and opinions about leadership.

GOOD DOG!

Using the word leadership is like saying "dog." People think they heard and understand what you said, but everyone pictures something different. Sometimes I use that example when working with a group. I tell them to imagine they are on a team and the team leader calls them together to explain the team's mission.

He says, *"Okay folks, this team's mission is to focus on dog. I want everyone to be working on dog. Got it?"*

The group salutes, agrees and goes to work. But, as time goes on, the team is not getting much done. The frustrated leader calls them back together. *"Can't you people do anything right? I gave you specific instructions to focus on dog and you are doing all kinds of different things."*

Then I ask a few people what pops into their heads when they hear the word dog. I get everything from Great Danes to Beagles. I even had one person say the word dog reminded him of his cat.

LEADERSHEEP

We have all heard stories about tribes that live near the Equator and have no words for snow, while those who live in colder regions have many words for snow. We are stuck with the language we have. There is a saying that *"We don't describe the world we see. We see the world we can describe."* Our language defines our world, including leadership.

We've got more definitions for leadership than an Alaskan has for snow. There is an almost infinite number of leadership approaches — from Great Danes to Beagles. If a word means everything, it really means nothing. It seems to me that leadership has become almost a meaningless term. You may be reading this thinking, *"Well, that is crazy. I know what leadership is."* We all have a vivid picture in our minds of leadership. But, as we have discussed, everyone's brain sees the world differently.

In one of our church meetings someone had a slip of the tongue — I think — and said "leadersheep" instead of leadership. As it turns out that is a pretty good definition of what some people want. *"We will be the sheep. You be the shepherd. You tell us what to do. We will just hang out here on the commons and munch some grass. Not baaaaaad."* Of course, when it comes time for shearing or providing a little lamb stew maybe being the sheep is not all that great.

When the man at church asked me, *"What do you think leadership is?"* I didn't want to say, *"Well, that is a really deep and interesting question and needs to be addressed in the context of a particular group and their situation vis à vis the larger multi-minded human system and blah blah blah."*

So I said, *"Leadership begins with a vision and ends with results."* If I were answering this question now, using our Four Levels glasses, I could say, *"Leadership begins at Level 4 and ends at Level 1."* Leadership begins with beliefs and ends in something created.

I didn't make up my response on the spot. I'm sure I'd heard or read something similar. There's a lot left unsaid in this quote, but, in our sound-bite world, you've got to have a quick response.

THE NEXT 10 WORDS

As President Bartlett said on one of the *West Wing* episodes, *"The important thing is the next ten words."* He was talking about the depth of someone's knowledge on big issues. It is easy to give a sound bite. What is underneath it is more important. Those are always longer, more difficult conversations.

That is certainly true for the term leadership. Just look back over the last couple years' worth of *Harvard Business Review, Fortune* or any other popular business magazine. There are many articles about "What Makes A Great Leader" or "The Five Styles of Leadership" or "The Seven Deadly Sins of Leadership."

Many of these articles can be helpful as starting points for our own leadership conversations. None of them is the complete answer to What is Leadership?

COUNTING SQUARES AND BUILDING LEADERS

Let's take the problem of defining leadership one step deeper by considering the diagram of the squares on page 55. How many squares are in that graphic? Usually, people say 16. Then, as they look closer and notice the larger squares, the number goes up.

Count them up. It's not that hard. What is your number? 16? 25? 30? 45?

Is there one correct answer?

How did you come up with your answer? Here is one approach.

Locate all the 1x1 squares. I see sixteen squares.

Now add in all the 2x2 squares: three on the bottom, three in the middle, three on the top.

That is nine more squares. Now add in the four 3x3 squares.

Don't forget the big overall 4x4 square. We located 16+9+4+1= 30 squares.

From this we can derive a formula. The next time someone asks you to figure out how many squares are in a figure with "X" squares along one side, in this case X=4, just apply the magic formula. That is: $(1)^2 + (2)^2 + (3)^2 \ldots (X)^2$ = total number of squares.

If we have a similar problem but now the figure contains five squares along each side, how many total squares are there? I hear those of you who are thinking clearly immediately say "55."

Question: Why was the harder problem easier to solve?

Answer: You knew the formula. You didn't have to do any creative thinking.

The how many squares question is a convergent problem. That is, the solution converges to one right answer. Thinking back to college, most of the problems given to us during our engineering education were convergent problems. They were sometimes difficult problems. But if you applied the correct formulas and didn't make any math errors — two really big ifs in my case — you could plug and chug and get the answer. I've heard others say that is how you get A's on tests.

"Yes, yes", you say. *"Big deal. So what"?* The big deal for me is that, until I was well out of college, I thought all problems were convergent problems. My attitude was, give me enough data and the right formulas and I can solve anything.

If that is true, why don't we just write the equation for leadership, plug in the numbers and solve for who does and who does not exhibit the best leadership? Why doesn't this work? Because the problem of defining leadership is a fundamentally different kind of problem. It does not have an answer like a math problem does.

The Myth of the Right Answer

This thought path leads us to Dr. Deming's System of Profound Knowledge. Deming advocated that managers study and understand four areas: theory of psychology, theory of systems, theory of variation and theory of knowledge.

Solving our how many squares problem takes us into the theory of knowledge. I first got some insight into the theory of knowledge at the 1995 Ohio Quality and Productivity Forum in Cincinnati. This annual meeting was put on by volunteers who studied and advanced Deming's ideas. That year Dr. John T. Edelman, a philosophy professor, gave a talk that caused a paradigm shift for me. I saw the world differently after he was done.

Two Types of Knowledge

He began by explaining two types of knowledge: a priori and empirical. A priori knowledge is a necessary truth, such as "a triangle has three sides." A priori knowledge is a sure thing — like our squares formula. Empirical knowledge is predictive based on experience, observation or experiment. As such it is probable only — not a sure thing. That is, the past does not guarantee the future. Dr. Deming said, *"Management is prediction and prediction is not certain."*

All Problems Are Not Created Equal

Professor Edelman said that problems lie on a continuum with 100% convergent problems on one end and 100% divergent problems on the other end. To solve a problem, first we need to understand the kind of problem it is because the two different kinds — convergent and divergent — require fundamentally different approaches.

As we have seen, convergent problems can be solved by the application of a rule or formula. Once you know the rule you can solve the problem without recreating the intellectual effort it took to develop the rule. Just "plug and chug." There is one right answer. Thank goodness for that.

Let's define some points along the convergent / divergent continuum. Counting the squares is a convergent problem. What about baking a loaf of bread? Where would that lie?

Let's say I have my favorite recipe for pumpernickel. I will give you the recipe, so you should have no problem consistently making that bread so it tastes just like the bread that I love from that little German bakery. At first, baking bread sounds like a convergent problem — follow the recipe — plug and chug.

A Pinch of This, a Dash of That

If you have ever tried to bake bread you know that task differs from solving the how many squares problem. For starters, it is not an abstract exercise. Baking bread involves *making* something in addition to *knowing* something.

There are also variables such as the yeast, the flour, the oven and the temperature and humidity of the kitchen.

And then, there's the baker — a major variable, or divergent element. Clearly, the odds of getting perfect bread every time after you have the recipe are lower than the odds of getting the correct answer to the how many squares problem after you know the formula.

Baking bread requires empirical knowledge, involves making something and includes a human. As such it is probable and therefore not a sure thing. Baking bread is closer to the divergent end of the scale than solving the how many squares problem.

Leadership In A Box

How about the problem of defining the term leadership for the twenty-first century? Where does that fall on the convergent / divergent continuum? Our first approach might be to distill out the common qualities of great leaders. Which leaders? In what types of situations? Will those same qualities work in a different setting and a different time in history?

Hartman's Glasses

We discussed Dr. Robert Hartman's Value Profile model earlier. It can be used to evaluate anything, including leadership. Put your Hartman glasses on for a minute and look at leadership through those lenses. Recall that Robert Hartman's three dimensions of value — intrinsic, extrinsic and systemic — involve people, things and ideas, in that order. Hartman said that people are more important than things and things are more important than concepts. A good leader, or a good person, would honor that order. An evil leader would reverse the order of importance. Continue to look at leadership using your Hartman glasses. If we believe leadership can be defined by an equation, we are taking a systemic view of leadership. The systemic dimension deals with mental concepts and theories: black and white, without any grays. From a systemic viewpoint, you are or aren't a leader. A leader is this and not that. The systemic dimension begs for a convergent answer.

Leadership, as we have been discussing it, is a larger, more amorphous, entity with many possibilities. An extrinsic view of leadership is what is found in much of the literature. The extrinsic view sees this style as better than that style. It says do these six things for effective leadership. The extrinsic dimension deals with the cause and effect world of comparisons and what is happening today.

Both the systemic and extrinsic definitions of leadership, while helpful, seem incomplete.

A richer intrinsic view would see leadership as personal, unique to each individual, with an infinite list of descriptors and possibilities. This type of leadership can only be understood by exploring and understanding that infinite list. The intrinsic view treats leadership as the divergent concept that it is.

WHERE'S MY RECIPE BOOK?

Clearly there is no formula for leadership. There is no rule or recipe that can be applied in rote fashion. You cannot even imagine a recipe, or, for that matter, you cannot understand the true nature of the question, "What is leadership?" if you have not thought about it deeply for some time. This is a predominantly divergent problem. Divergent problems cannot be solved by mere technique — they require knowledge.

Our speaker that day in Cincinnati defined art as the ability to produce something based on knowledge. Only knowledge transforms skill into art. Only art can hope to deal with the novelty that is an inevitable part of life.

That is why you should be suspicious of anyone who wants to give you *The Five Qualities of Great Leaders*, or any variation on that theme, with the implication that if you emulate those five qualities you will be a great leader. That approach implies a recipe exists. It implies there is a convergent solution to this divergent problem. And, it implies you can solve this problem without investing the intellectual effort to understand the problem.

There is no "Leadership In A Box."

That's not to say that *The Five Qualities of Great Leaders* is useless. If you study those same five qualities as one stop on your journey of figuring out how to express your own leadership in the world, then you are learning. Divergent problems require learning and this can be one of many useful exercises. You may be thinking, *"Let me get this straight. Most of the problems we deal with in organizations are divergent. Divergent problems don't have an answer. Therefore, we're doomed."*

It may sound like we are doomed, but once you understand how to deal with divergent problems, you will become even more effective.

THE OPPOSITE IS ALSO TRUE

There are two keys to taking on divergent problems. The first key is to look for the opposites. Underneath most divergent problems you will find a tug of what at first looks like opposites, or paradox. Learning the art of identifying and balancing opposites is necessary to dealing with divergent problems.

The art of balancing opposites requires that you understand the problem deeply enough to recognize that within the statement of the problem is the beginning of the conversation leading to a solution.

For example, we looked at the concept of freedom through control. At first, these terms sound like opposites. We think it must be either freedom or control. In fact, this concept can be a way to allow people to improve processes (freedom) while keeping variation to a minimum (control.) We might begin the conversation by asking how control and freedom can be balanced to create better results.

As a simple example, a client wanted to involve the staff more in the running of the business, but did not want to end run the managers. They decided to focus on cross-departmental issues that needed solving and were not within any one department's sphere of influence. The first year they created teams to deal with these issues, with the managers as team leaders. The next year staff members acted as leaders with the managers as advisors. Now some of the teams work with very little direct manager involvement. This approach has also given some of the staff people more leadership opportunities to grow and develop. This is not a particularly unusual example, but it shows how a shift in thinking can create new realities and opportunities.

A quote attributed to Oliver Wendell Holmes, an associate justice on the United States Supreme Court from 1902 to 1932, applies here: *"I wouldn't give a fig for the simplicity on this side of complexity but I would give my right arm for the simplicity on the far side of complexity."*

YOU DON'T KNOW WHAT YOU DON'T KNOW

This brings up the second key to working with divergent problems. You need to be at least somewhat comfortable with the idea of not knowing. Not knowing is crucial to thinking about the tension between your current best practices and finding a better approach. If you believe you already know the answer, you will be more likely to defend that answer.

The idea of not knowing brings up its own control versus freedom issues in organizations and may, paradoxically, become the block to new knowing. There is an unspoken belief in many organizations about a need for control and being in control is what many people expect from their leaders. The paradox here is that, if control equals knowing and not in control equals not knowing then the people who develop new solutions to problems will be the ones who don't know. And yet, what is valued in many organizations are experts or those that know. How do we get to the simplicity on the far side of that complexity?

"Beginner's mind" may be a better term than not knowing. This is a phrase coined by Shunryu Suzuki, founder of the San Francisco Zen Center, to explain the process of inquiry while meditating. A beginner's mind does not know the answer and is therefore open to new answers. Or, to quote Suzuki Roshi, *"In the beginner's mind there are many possibilities, but in the expert's mind there are few."*

MEANWHILE, BACK AT THE CHURCH

When the gentleman at the church asked me what leadership was, maybe I should have said that was the wrong question. Asking "what is leadership?" is like asking who the president of the Internet is. There isn't one. A better question for the church committee might have been, *"How can we balance the boundaries and traditions of this religion with the freedom to create a parish that is right for us?"* That question would have required knowledge, but that knowledge was available within the group.

IT'S PERSONAL

Instead, I said, *"Leadership begins with a vision and ends with results."*

"Well," the man at the church said to me, *"I agree with the vision part."*

Rarely in organizations does one person with a great idea bring it to reality by him or her self. Most results are created interdependently, rather than independently. Leadership is more than just the vision part, or else we believe there is one royal smart person who provides the vision and all the Theory X workers create the results.

What I am saying is that every individual needs to have a personal vision — a clear mental picture of what he or she wants to create in this life. And he or she needs to be working — taking action — creating results — to move closer to that self-direction.

There is a personal side, as well as a social side, to leadership. That is why this assumption about everyone being a leader is in the personal part of The Page. If a person does not first recognize and embrace his own responsibility to lead his own life, it is unlikely that he will have the internal drive to fulfill his social leadership obligations.

The movie *Rudy* is a great example of personal leadership. You may have seen this classic. The movie tells the story of a young man named Rudy, who dreamed of playing football at Notre Dame despite some physical shortcomings. He held that dream in his head from the time he was five years old until the day he actually walked onto the field as a member of the Fighting Irish football team. In the interim, Rudy endured numerous setbacks to his dream, which became just the next hurdle to overcome on the way to the football field.

The two aspects of leadership — future vision and present work — are also captured in Robert Hartman's model. You may want to glance back at the table in Chapter Two while you slip those glasses on once more. Hartman defined both an external and an internal world. Each world consists of three separate dimensions of value.

Self-Direction, the *internal systemic* dimension of his model, measures how a person values her future. Does she have a clear positive mental image of her future? If so, she will likely have a lot of energy to pursue that future. This is where personal vision begins.

Role Awareness, the *internal extrinsic* dimension of Hartman's model, measures how a person values what she is doing in the present to move herself toward her desired future — today's results. Your being is your becoming.

These two dimensions form the personal side of leadership. The mental creation always precedes the physical creation. Both are necessary.

Rudy knew what he wanted and what he had to do to get it. First he had a very clear and positive understanding of his own self-direction — where he was headed. He also had a clear view of his role as a Notre Dame football player. Rudy was a Notre Dame football player in his head, long before he put on the uniform. The external world kept intruding. It was his internal clarity and fire that kept him on his path despite setbacks. It was Rudy's persistence that kept him doing whatever he needed to move closer to his goal. This is the personal side of leadership.

Rudy knew he was a Notre Dame football player when he was five years old. The rest was just detail.

PLENTY FOR EVERYBODY

Leadership is not a zero-sum commodity. What if leadership in an organization gets widely distributed throughout the whole, as we were attempting to do in the church? Everyone takes some ownership for part of the whole, a piece of the mission, as well as caring about others involved in the mission. Everyone leads where they have some influence.

This idea comes from Robert Greenleaf, writing in his 1991 book *The Servant as Leader*. Speaking of leadership as a service to others, Greenleaf says:

> *"It begins with the natural feeling that one wants to serve, to serve first. Then conscious choice brings one to aspire to lead... The difference manifests itself in the care taken by the servant — first to make sure that other people's highest priority needs are being served. Do those served grow as persons; do they, while being served, become healthier, wiser, freer, more autonomous, more likely themselves to be servants? And what is the effect on the least privileged in society; will he or she benefit, or at least, will he or she not be further deprived?"*

This quote turns many notions about leadership upside down and begs the question for all of us, *"Why do I want to lead? Is it for me or for others?"*

THE GOOD LEADER

I have moved the conversation beyond the personal to the social aspect of leadership. When a person begins to see himself as closely connected to others, when he begins to open the boundaries between himself and the rest of the world, he is changing and enlarging his self concept and will be better able to serve and lead others.

For leadership to spread virally, it takes the previously mentioned assumptions from *The Page*. In particular, it requires individuals working together with shared vision to create something greater than what they could have created on their own. They need some control over how they do their work and they need to understand why that work is important. They need to be doing work that suits their behavioral profile and is intrinsically motivating to them. And this is just at the individual level. We will talk about other enablers at the culture and organization levels in later chapters.

ROLL YOUR OWN LEADERSHIP

As we look back over these thoughts on leadership — combined with the elegant uniqueness of humans — we find an infinite number of leadership paths possible for people, with a wide spectrum of effectiveness and outcomes. The tapestry that people weave of their lives and their legacies is made up of many threads. Individual talents, how that talent is expressed, parents, training, background, upbringing, chance opportunities and setbacks, the response to those events, karma, etc. all contribute to what constitutes the results of a person's life and the legacy of their personal leadership. Talk about a divergent problem!

Will they be good leaders? That is the question. How would we know? Answering that question takes prediction. Prediction implies probabilities. Probabilities mean uncertainty. I hope we all become good leaders.

Underneath this whole discussion, "know thyself" is still great advice. However a person leads, it must be from who he is. His authenticity legitimizes his personal leadership. Who he is will create what he does and how people respond to it.

THE QUESTION PROVIDES THE ANSWER

As I mentioned above, questions involving divergent problems often contain opposing ideas: control versus freedom, the individual versus the group, do what you want versus do what is needed, top down versus bottom up, etc.

The questions around how to balance those opposites are where solutions and conversations get interesting. Talking together about how to deal with those opposites and create desirable results is an important conversation.

LEADING THE LEADERS

At our church, considering the "How do we do that?" question was probably the most important thing we did to move the idea of shared leadership ahead.

One thing that came from these conversations was a decision to meet informally every couple of weeks on Saturday mornings. These meetings were open to anyone who was chairing a committee or doing any other leadership — and those who wanted to do something.

At these bi-weekly meetings we discussed a topic that was important to the participants, such as how to deal with committee members who don't follow through on assignments, or how to balance the conversation between the extroverts and introverts, or how to hold volunteers accountable. These were great conversations in the spirit of beginner's mind and we all grew from them.

The role of Head Rector or General Manager may have, in Dr. Stephen Covey's terms, a larger circle of influence than someone else in the organization. Maybe she gets paid more than others. Perhaps she has the most positional power. Usually some decisions can only be made by the person "at the top." She may also be legally accountable for some things that cannot be dealt with by anyone else in the organization.

The above characteristics of the top dog do not mean others are NOT also leaders. Everyone can be, should be and is a leader. If nothing else, we all lead our lives, for better or worse.

I am not saying to turn over the asylum to the inmates. I am suggesting that deciding who is responsible for what in this organization is a divergent problem. The question of how to deal with the apparent opposites of sharing leadership throughout the organization while staying on course deserves a thoughtful conversation in every organization.

TALKING ABOUT VALUES

The concept we explored earlier about the Four Levels of system thinking will become apparent when having these conversations. The values and beliefs of the people in charge of the organization are found in Level 4. Typically, these values are tacit and not specifically discussed.

Conversations regarding personal leadership will make some of these values more apparent with questions such as:

- What does personal dignity mean in this organization?
- What do we believe about differences between managers and non-managers, exempt and non-exempt, factory and front office, first shift and "off shift?" Do we intend to use these artificial differences to create an upper and lower class? Are we?

- If part of every leader's job is to increase the capacity and leadership capability of others in the organization, what would our organization look like if every person were a leader?

- Do we see this organization as a machine made up of individual parts, or do we see this organization as a living system containing many divergent human elements? What does this difference mean to us in terms of leadership?

- How do we balance the need for one leader at the top with diffused leadership throughout the organization? What does this decision imply?

Managers and others lead these conversations in organizations that are willing to think deeply about the beliefs that were used to create the organization.

Role of Management

Any task requiring the cooperative efforts of humans, including service, production, sales and management is predominately a divergent problem, if only because of a human's inherent free will and the need to create something, let alone all the other variables.

A manager who has not considered the two types of knowledge, a priori and empirical, may hold people accountable for future solutions that may not exist. During the philosophy professor's lecture, he commented that many managers *"...do not recognize the probable character of the predictive element in empirical knowledge when they hold individuals responsible for the various tasks assigned to them."*

This is apparent in conversations such as:

"Can you guarantee that you will meet next year's quota?"

"Oh sure, no problem."

"Good, I'd hate to have to fire you."

We've explored two concepts in this chapter: personal leadership and the divergent nature of much of our work. In light of these ideas, what should be the role of management in an organization of leaders working on divergent problems? By now you should recognize a divergent question when you hear one.

I suggest that the era when the manager's job was to plan, organize and control is quickly drawing to a close. If we believe that the organization runs on interdependence and relationships, then the manager's prime task becomes building interdependence and relationships, both within his group and with other groups across the organization.

Barry Oshry explains this concept in his book *Seeing Systems*. He talks about an organization with Tops, Middles and Bottoms as different types of positions in the organization. In most organizations the Middles spend all their time working up to satisfy bosses, working down to satisfy their work group, or feeling torn apart in the middle, between those two groups. This leaves no time for working where their real leverage lies; working across, with other Middles, integrating what needs to happen across the organization. This Middle Integration, as Oshry calls it, rarely happens for a number of predictable reasons: competition for promotions, nothing in common with those other middles, not enough time, etc. However, when a structure is put in place to encourage communication and interaction, the Middle becomes a valuable member of the organization, filling a unique role as integrator that no other position can do as effectively.

There is an old adage that says, *"Manage processes, lead people."* What if that became the job of the manager? Hold the organization's vision and help create the results by making it easier for what needs to happen to happen.

So what?

There are many different styles of effective leadership. These intrinsic human capacities are not bestowed on someone at the time of promotion. They are inside each person, waiting to be discovered, developed and used. Excellent organizations are places where people are encouraged to practice and perfect their talents in a variety of ways that serve themselves, others and the organization.

The leadership equation does not have one right answer. We can't even write the equation, let alone solve it. When individual leadership, in all its variations, is nourished and developed, both the individual and the organization benefit.

Now What?

1. Do you have a clear positive mental image of something you want to create in your future? If not, you might want to take the time to create a mental picture of your perfect day, five to ten years from now, and then summarize that picture in a few paragraphs. Don't rush this exercise. Describe your perfect future with enough clarity that we would recognize it if we saw it. Work out of your imagination, not your memory.

2. Once you have completed a description of your future ask yourself each week, "What action am I taking this week to move myself closer to my vision?"

3. Who are you as a leader? Ask yourself, "What type of leader am I?" If a movie were made about your leadership style would you be the king, the general, the teacher, the servant, the shaman, the parent, the savior?

4. What other types of leaders are waiting inside you to be discovered?

5. On a scale of 0-10 where would you put your current level of personal leadership?
   0 = The leader is not home
   10 = My influence is larger than I ever thought

6. Are you satisfied with that number at this time? If not, what behavior could you stop doing, start doing, or change to increase your leadership number?

7. What will your Page say about personal leadership?

PART TWO

CULTURE

The first part of *The Page* has been about individuals. Individuals come together and animate organizations. To refer to Max DePree's quote, *"An organization cannot be anything its people are not."* The good news is people can be great. Everyone deserves to be treated intrinsically as the unique human being and great leader that he or she can be. My belief is that most of the people in our organizations want to do well and succeed. Their success depends on their behavior and their behavior is affected by how they see their world and themselves. To that extent, every organization is dealt the same hand.

We will next look at the Culture and then the Systemic Parts of the organization to see if we can develop some assumptions about why — if every organization is dealt the same hand — we get such wildly different results.

Culture exists in the relationships between individuals and at the interface between individuals and the organization. One of the best explanations of culture that I have found comes from page 2 of Daniel Denison's book, *Corporate Culture and Organizational Effectiveness*:

> *"Culture refers to the underlying values, beliefs and principles that serve as a foundation for an organization's management system as well as the set of management practices and behaviors that both exemplify and reinforce those basic principles. These principles and practices endure because they have meaning for the members of an organization. They represent strategies for survival that have worked well in the past and that the members believe will work well again in the future. Thus a cultural theory of organizational effectiveness must take as its starting point the observation that the values, beliefs and meanings that underlie a social system are the primary source of motivated and coordinated activity."*

Culture is a strong influence on behavior and therefore of results. Put an individual in culture #1 get C– results. Put the same person in culture #2, get A+ results. Same person, different results. Part Two, the Culture section of *The Page*, lists my three assumptions about why this happens. These key assumptions focus on trust, competition and feedback.

THE PAGE

Our work with clients is based on the following assumptions. Everyone does not hold these beliefs. We list them so people we work with will know what to expect from us.

ABOUT INDIVIDUALS:

- Each individual is unique. He or she values ideas, things and people differently and responds to challenges differently. When individuals work together these differences can create chaos or synergy.
- People choose their behavioral responses to what happens to them and are therefore responsible for their own beha_____ _____ think of based on internal and external _____ _____ may or may not be effective.

> *A high-trust working environment will create better short and long-term results than a low-trust working environment.*

- Most people want to do well an_____ _____ they do their work, and understand wh_____
- Leadership resides in every person. It is not reserved _____ for executives and managers.

ABOUT THE CULTURE:

- *A high-trust working environment will create better short and long-term results than a low-trust working environment.*
- People need feedback from processes, customers, suppliers and employees of an organization so they can improve. Facts, data and the scientific method provide feedback. Judgment and blame are not feedback.
- *An organization is an interdependent system. Competition within a culture creates winners and losers, artificial scarcity and loss. It does not help the organization. Competition between independent organizations is acceptable.*

ABOUT ORGANIZATIONS:

- Every organization is perfectly designed to _____ _____ over 85% of the problems experienced by o_____ structure, policies, procedures, etc. and N_____

> *An organization in an interdependent system. Competition within a culture creates winners and losers, artificial scarcity and loss. It does not help the organization. Competition between independent organizations is acceptable.*

- Organizations and individuals grow an_____ of and improve the assets and resour_____ stakeholders.
- An organization stays in existence bec_____ suppliers, employees, owners and the _____ the relationship.

TRUST AND COMPETITION

CHAPTER 5

THE PAGE

A high-trust working environment will create better short and long-term results than a low-trust working environment.

An organization is an interdependent system. Competition within an organization creates winners and losers, artificial scarcity and loss. It does not help the organization. Competition between independent organizations is acceptable.

TRUST ME

In the classic *Charlie Brown* cartoon strips Lucy holds the football while Charlie Brown runs at it for all he is worth to kick it. At the last second, just as he is about to boot the ball, Lucy pulls the football back. Charlie Brown's foot kicks nothing. He flies through the air and lands flat on his back — every time.

Charlie Brown always trusts Lucy and she always betrays his trust. If Charlie Brown ever stumbled into the *Dilbert* comic strip by mistake, Dilbert would surely explain to Charlie Brown how he should not be so gullible.

Most of us aren't as trusting as Charlie Brown. We have all these sayings, such as:

Fool me once, shame on you — Fool me twice, shame on me.

Look before you leap (or kick a football).

In God we trust. All others bring data.

Trust Allah, but tie your camel.

When I facilitated workshops based on Dr. Stephen Covey's *The Seven*

Habits of Highly Effective People, I often used a game based on "The Prisoner's Dilemma" to illustrate Habit 4, Think Win-Win or No Deal. The Prisoner's Dilemma is well known in game theory. We called our game "Win As Much As You Can." I found it to be an effective way to focus people on how quickly trust can affect a culture.

WIN AS MUCH AS YOU CAN GAME — THE SETUP

In our game people played for the best score, tallied in imaginary dollars. Imagine a room with sixteen people in four groups of four people each. Call them groups A, B, C and D. The game is simple to learn to play. I would explain to the participants that:

- This game consists of a number of rounds of play;
- We will play one round at a time;
- Each group will select either an X or a Y for each round;
- Each group will strategize and make their choice in private with the other members of their group;
- Talking between groups is not allowed;
- After all four groups have made their choices in private, the four groups will simultaneously reveal their choices; and
- Each group's choice combined with the choices of the other groups will be used to calculate the score for that round.

After that brief introduction I would give the four groups a few minutes to look over their scoring options and come up with their strategy for the first round. The scorecard was set up for ten rounds.

THE SCORE CARD

What they saw on their score cards is what you see in the table below. If all four groups vote Y, all groups get rewarded (+$1). The catch is that if one of the groups decides to vote X, that group wins $3 for that round while the other groups lose $1 each.

SCORING	PAYOFFS
0 groups vote X, 4 groups vote Y	Ys win $1 each
1 group votes X, 3 groups vote Y	X wins $3, Ys lose $1 each
2 groups vote X, 2 groups vote Y	Xs win $2 each, Ys lose $2 each
3 groups vote X, 1 group votes Y	Xs win $1 each, Y loses $3
4 groups vote X, 0 groups vote Y	Xs lose $1 each

Some groups saw immediately that all Ys was the only way for the larger group — the entire room — to prosper. Any X turned the game into a zero sum game or worse. Others saw X as the only viable vote, to limit their risk and not be taken advantage of by another group. Perhaps some strategy drifted into your head as you looked over the scoring.

THE GOAL AND THE PROCESS

Before the groups began I wrote the goal on a chart: Goal: Win as much as you can. That appeared to be a simple sentence with a clear meaning, until each person's own version of what "win" means and who "you" is made for a lively game. A ten-round game took about 30 minutes to play.

If you have played this game, what follows will bring back memories. For those of you who have not had the pleasure, I have included a mock scorecard at the back of this chapter to help you understand what typically happens. You may want to refer to it during the following explanation.

LET THE GAMES BEGIN! — ROUND 1

Each group and game develops its own culture. In the first round typically one or more of the groups will vote X, maybe as a guess because they haven't figured things out, maybe as a defensive vote to protect themselves. If all four groups vote to protect themselves the larger group is $4 poorer.

The groups that voted Y — we'll just call them Ys for simplicity — shake their heads at the stupidity of the Xs and hope they wise up by Round 2. The Xs mark up a dollar or two on their score sheet.

TIME FOR STRATEGY — ROUND 2

In Round 2 the tally is often three Xs and one Y. I announce, *"Minus three dollars for the Y group."* Someone in an X group laughs at the misfortune and / or stupidity of the Ys. Comments are made. I reinstate the no communicating rule — and add, *"No name-calling, please."* Amazingly, the tone in the room begins to change. Competitive people don't like to be laughed at and they don't like to lose. After about five minutes into this game being played for imaginary dollars (and ego), each group is now actively engaged in strategizing.

FROM BAD TO WORSE — ROUNDS 3 AND 4

All this strategy work often yields four Xs in Round 3. *"Minus $1 each, get* *ready to play Round 4"* I say. Now what? Each group knows the chances are slim to none that all three other groups will switch to Y. And, if that does not happen, they must vote X to protect themselves. But if all four groups use this impeccable logic, round four will look a lot like Round 3.

It is still early in the game. Scores are low. One team will be ahead by a dollar or two. That team thinks, *"We might not have much, but we can stay ahead of the others."* And their definition of win as much as you can becomes having a better score than the other groups — even if that score is negative.

We play Round 4 and, big surprise, four Xs. The room is sinking deeper into the red, with no obvious way out. The mood becomes darker. If I ask who is at fault, everyone blames another group. Very few see that they have any part in creating these unwanted results.

A Way Out...

After Round 4 I ask if anyone would like to temporarily suspend the no-talking rule and meet with people in another group before they mark the next round — Round 5. Usually they say, *"Yes."* Sometimes someone will say, *"What for? You can't trust them."*

Amazingly, after about ten minutes into a game played for essentially no stakes, well-educated, professional, relatively sane people are actually angry enough at each other and so distrustful that they don't see any hope in conversation. When I see this I am always amazed that the world is not more screwed up.

Conversations are short, a couple of minutes goes by. They explain to each other that Y is the only way to prosperity. Obviously, we should all mark Y. Yes, I agree, etc. They retreat to their own groups. *"No more inter-group talking,"* I say. They prepare to mark their choices for Round 5.

Or Not — Round 5

When talking with the other groups, people usually make some commitment to mark a Y. But when people get back in their own group to confirm this strategy and mark their card for Round 5, skullduggery happens. At this point I let them know that Round 5 is a bonus round. That is, all scores, both plus and minus, will be multiplied by three. That fact is also on their score cards. The pressure is too much for some groups. They vote an X. Scores are revealed. Those who voted Y are offended beyond measure at the infidelity of the Xs. The Xs cheer nervously and congratulate themselves on their wily play.

Every now and then something different happens in Round 5. All four groups mark Y. *"Plus $3 for each group,"* I say. There is a different kind of celebration. Everyone feels good and shares the feeling. The energy shifts. Round 6 follows and it is even more rare that all four groups continue to all mark Y. Sometimes it happens. Usually there are one or two groups who mark X in Round 6 and that puts the room back on the downward spiral.

THE ACTION CREATES THE CULTURE

In the situation where all four groups mark Y in Round 6, (+$1 for each group) the mood considerably lightens. The time between rounds shortens, as there is no need for complex strategy. People begin to trust each other more and therefore they begin to see the game differently. What "win" means and who "you" is take on different meanings. The four competitive groups become cooperative in a way they thought not possible ten minutes earlier. It is a rare but beautiful sight.

The game continues for ten rounds. Rounds 8 and 10 are also bonus rounds. I offer inter-group conversation before each of these rounds. It's not unusual that the groups are so angry with each other that they don't want to talk before these rounds. There are many variations in play possible.

FROM PARTICIPANTS TO OBSERVERS

A debrief follows the game. I let the group do as much of the talking as possible. *"What happened here?"* I ask and that is enough to launch a spirited 15-20 minute conversation.

WE HAVE MET THE ENEMY...

"It was your fault, Randy, you told us to compete with each other." (That is why I always write the goal on a chart where everyone can see it before we play.)

"When did I tell you to compete?" I ask.

"You said <u>Win</u> as much as you can!"

"What does "Win" mean to you?"

"You know — it means win," they say, with a tone that implies I must be really stupid.

"Oh, win — like in beat the other teams?"

"Well, yes, I guess — yes, beat the other teams."

Many times all four groups end up with a minus score after Xing each other for several rounds. Even if a team manages to stay above $0, they earn a lot less than what is theoretically possible: $125 in a ten-round game.

"So, your team has minus $5. You call that winning?" I ask.

"We didn't do as bad as those other guys," they respond defensively.

If I am feeling really ornery I say something like, *"The goal doesn't say 'Lose as little as possible' Were you confused? Your division lost 5 million dollars last year. And, even though the other three divisions lost more, I'm sorry to have to tell you we are closing all four divisions. You'll get your last check today,"* I intone with mock seriousness.

"No, No! It's not like that. We weren't four divisions like in our own company. We were competitors."

"How did you determine that?" I ask.

The more thoughtful people begin to ponder the idea of who "you" is in their real life. Win as much as <u>you</u> can. What if you includes everyone in the room — all four groups?

In fact, that is the shift that occurs to the people who end up Ying for each other. The circle of who is us expands a little. Their thinking moves from independent to interdependent. Maybe every interaction does not need to be a competition.

WHEN TO COMPETE

"When should you compete and when should you not?" I ask. I posed this question to a group of MBA students recently and one young man sarcastically told me the answer to when not to compete was found in "The Loser's Handbook" (I have not listed *that* as a reference). For many people competition is the normal state and, for some people, the only state they know.

I push on, *"Is this game an independent or an interdependent activity?"* I ask. We figure out that the game is interdependent because of the rules. When one group marks an X or a Y, that action affects the other groups' scores. Inter means between or among or in the midst of or reciprocal. The game's scoring rules establish a reciprocal dependence among the four groups.

Groups may choose to play the game independently, as if looking out for themselves is all that matters. This gets them into trouble every time. The game is an interdependent reality, no matter how they choose to play. As Pogo, the comic strip possum of the 1940s, famously said, *"We have met the enemy and he is us."*

As we dive deeper into the idea of competition — winners and losers — versus cooperation — helping everyone achieve their best — we discover that in those cases of interdependence, where your outcome depends on my action and vice versa, a win-lose strategy is ultimately a lose-lose strategy.

At this point in the debrief some participants consider the idea that perhaps competition within interdependent groups might be counterproductive.

WE'RE ALL IN THE SAME BOAT

I saw a wonderful cartoon. The picture shows two men in a small rowboat, one sitting at each end. There is a hole in one end, with water shooting up between the legs of one of the men and that end of the boat is sinking. The man at the other end says *"I'm sure glad the hole is in your end of the boat."*

People in organizations, like the men in the cartoon, are in the same boat. An organization is an interdependent system. It is a place where there is a reciprocal reliance on each other for support and existence. What occurs in one part affects the other parts. Shake one part of a spider web and the whole web vibrates. Injure one part of a living system and you injure the whole. Put a hole in one end of a boat... .

And yet, think about how many competitive policies, structures, systems and beliefs are found in interdependent organizations. The 100% sales club, the guideline that only 10% of the workforce are rated 1s, the employee-of-the month parking space are a few simple examples. These artificial constructs create a culture of artificial scarcity. Many of these competitive structures are based on the well-meaning belief that, if you improve the parts, you improve the whole.

A counter belief and the one I subscribe to, is that you cannot understand the whole from the parts and indeed, to optimize the whole you may have to sub-optimize some of the parts.

A simple example of this way of thinking can be found in any well-run factory and is detailed in the book *The Goal*, by Eliahu Goldratt. In the old days manufacturing plants ran all their equipment to the maximum. The goal was to make as many parts on each machine as possible. The idea was that if a machine was sitting there and not making parts, it was wasting money. As it turns out, that is only part of the equation.

Some parts take longer to make than others. And, some parts are used in greater numbers than others. Plus, the assemblies that are built out of these parts have their own assembly times and they must be assembled into the final product. So in any plant there were piles of parts and assemblies being held as Work In Process (WIP). And, since Murphy is an optimist, no plant runs perfectly. When an error cropped up downstream, then some or all of that WIP upstream needed to be reworked or scrapped, wasting money. A machine that is busy making bad parts is wasting money.

Today most manufacturers understand that the efficiency of the factory is not measured at the machine level, but at the factory level. Having a machine standing idle instead of making unneeded parts makes sense in this factory.

SYSTEM THINKING

When working with managers I'll say something like, *"If we could collect the best transmission and the best engine and the best seats, etc. — all the best individual parts from the various automobile manufacturers around the globe — I'll bet we could make a really great car then."*

They laugh and wonder how they got stuck with such an idiot for a consultant. But then they go back to work and attempt to optimize each of their departments independently in the hopes of creating the best organization.

It is obviously important to have good parts, whatever those parts are. What is more important to the success of the whole than the individual parts is the relationships between the parts: how the parts work together to support the mission of the whole — another example of interdependence.

In high school biology class did you dissect the frog and find all the parts? Tough on the frog. In engineering school we learned how to analyze something by taking it apart and understanding the parts. That is often useful. If I am going to build a car it helps to know what roles the shocks and transmission play.

An equally-useful skill and one that got far less emphasis in school, is understanding through synthesis. If you had no idea what a car was to be used for, you would have to see the car in the context of the larger systems — roads, communities, etc. — before you fully understood the car and its purpose. Or, in the example of the manufacturing plant, we need to see each parts-making machine in the context of the whole production facility to really understand how it should be used.

There are many examples of a product or service finding increased usage after the product was considered within the larger system. Just look at all the uses for baking soda on the side of the box. How much genius is there in a product that, to use it, you have to dump it down the drain?

These two ideas: (1) the relationships between the parts are more important than the sum of the parts and (2) you can only fully understand a system by seeing it at both a higher (synthesis) and a lower (analysis) level, are both well-known concepts in system thinking. But these ideas are not widely accepted and practiced by many organizations.

I worked with a client who had similar operations in several locations. One location's measures of success were dropping. After extensive diagnosis we found a new position for that site's manager and identified three areas to work on: improving trust, reducing blame while increasing learning and renewing the focus on processes. The employees, the parts, stayed the same. A number of them formed teams to work on these three areas. The relationships between the parts (employees) started improving. Within a few months that location was back on track and making significant improvements, even before the next site manager arrived.

WHOSE SIDE ARE YOU ON?

When we talk about interdependent groups and competition, many people immediately think about competitive team sports. When the University of Kentucky Wildcats basketball team takes the floor at Rupp Arena, I want them thinking "win." In this sense they are acting independently against the other team.

The insight is that, in order to win, the team itself, an interdependent reality, must cooperate and optimize the relationships between the parts (players) in order for the team to excel. Basketball is an independent game played by two teams consisting of interdependent players. It takes great athletes to compete in today's NCAA division one game. And yet, many times the less talented team beats the one with the more individually talented players. That phenomenon sometimes occurs when a great individual performer is willing to suboptimize his or her individual performance for the good of the team.

At a higher level, say at the NCAA level, the teams are interdependent again, as they all adhere to and cooperate with the policies of the governing body for the benefit of all. For example, they all abide by the rules governing how tournament money is shared.

It is not unusual to hear about world class athletes who train with each other, helping each other to achieve higher levels of performance. Then, during a competition (say at an Olympic event) they compete against each other for the gold medal.

Ys Up

We have talked about how win-lose is not the best strategy for the Win As Much As You Can Game and, by extension, for any interdependent situation.

Lose-win is also not the best strategy. Who would choose lose-win in this game, you ask? Let's get back to the game debrief and look at those who marked Y. It is always interesting to watch those groups get great pleasure out of seeing the Xers get lectured about the flaws of the win-lose strategy.

So I turn to these Ys Guys, who usually have an even lower score since they marked more Ys (minus $3) than the Xers (+$1), (see Group D in the Normal Game scorecard on page 89) and I ask them how they did.

"Good," they say.

"Alright and what is your score again?"

"Minus $124."

And the Xers, what is their score?

"The worst ones are Group A, they have $60."

"What do you call it when you have less than the other guys?"

"Lose-Win?"

"Correct."

"Yeah, but that was because they marked X. It was not our fault. We tried to talk sense to them. They wouldn't listen. They screwed us on rounds 7 and 8."

And then we explore the idea that, if I know you are going to mark Y and I am biased toward independence and competing and winning, I will mark X. You will become my victim. Although you may know that marking Y is beneficial to all, if you cannot influence me to change my strategy, you will encourage me to continue to mark X and we will both lose in the long run.

Tit For Tat

What can the team that wants to mark Y do to keep from being taken advantage of? Robert Axelrod's book, *The Evolution of Cooperation*, describes a strategy employed by people who write software versions of these games to play against one another on computers. These computer programs are played for more than ten rounds, just like the real Win As Much As You Can games that we all play every day of our lives.

A strategy that fares very well against other strategies is known as "Tit For Tat." Basically, this software program always selects Y for the first round. It continues to mark Y unless its opponent marks X in any round. It then marks X the following round and continues marking X every round until the opponent switches to Y. When the Tit For Tat program sees a Y from the other program, it immediately returns the favor in the following rounds until it gets Xed again. Tit For Tat is simple for the other programs to figure out. It is predictable. And, it immediately makes the other program pay for Xing. Tit For Tat is both quick to act to defend itself and quick to forgive.

How could a team that wants to mark Y use Tit For Tat thinking in our Win As Much As You Can game? When they get a chance to talk to the other groups they can say something like, *"All Y's is the only strategy that lets us all make money. We promise to mark Y in the next round. We think all groups should mark Y. However, if any of the other three groups mark X in the next round or any round thereafter, we will X you back in the following round and continue to X until we see a Y from you. Again it is in all of our best interests to cooperate here. But, if you choose to not cooperate, we promise to not be your victim."*

The way I used to describe it during the debrief and what I learned from Dr. Covey, was, *"Be unconditionally trustworthy. Give trust conditionally."*

Going for a win-win strategy is not always easy and often requires courage. Win-win is a combination of courage and compassion. It takes courage to stand up for our win and not be taken advantage of. It takes compassion to see that the other person's win is also, in part, our responsibility. This mindset requires a level of maturity not found in every interaction. That is why Stephen Covey's admonition of "win-win *or no deal*" is so powerful. The no deal part is your guarantee that the other party will not victimize you.

TRUST ME

Trust, or the lack of it, plays a part in all relationships. In his book *The Wisdom of Crowds*, James Suroweicki describes how trust is implicit in many of the systems we take for granted. For example, trading on the stock market, driving on a crowded highway and paying taxes. If we don't trust the other people, or don't trust ourselves, or don't trust the system, or don't trust the circumstances, most of us do not go into that relationship full speed like Charlie Brown. We hold back, physically and emotionally. It may be an almost unconscious reaction. We have an innate desire to protect ourselves from ridicule or danger. No normal person wants to be taken advantage of, or made a fool of, or make a bad decision.

The willingness to give trust varies greatly among people. People also vary in how quickly they recover from having that trust violated and how a violation of trust in one aspect of their lives does or does not affect their ability to trust in other areas of their life.

In Chapter 3 I talked about the "Influence" component of a person's natural behavioral style. People who have a lot of this component in their behavioral style, the high Is, are more naturally extroverted, optimistic and trusting. Others with a lower Influence score appear more distrusting and introverted in their behavior.

Organizations are made up of a mixture of behavioral styles. No organization has all high I's. And, no organization automatically has a naturally high trust culture. Since every organization is created based on the founders' beliefs, every organization has rules and structures that either enhance or detract from the trust in that environment. This is an important point because, when it comes to creating results with others, trust is the lubricant for the human machine. Creating results is much easier in a high trust environment.

In the Win As Much As You Can game, the game gets a lot easier if and when the four groups begin to trust each other. The rounds go quicker because there is no need for complex strategies. (See The Game Less Played Scorecard) Similarly, people working in high-trust environments can focus 100% on creating results without having to focus on CYA.

Hand Me That Trustometer

How would you measure trust? There is not, as far as I know, an Acme Trustometer. Let's invent one. It looks like a cell phone, but the display has what looks like a little traffic light on it, with a red, yellow and green lights. Beside the lights the display reads:

- Red = Low (0-30%) trust. Proceed with great caution!

- Yellow = Medium (31-65%) trust. Okay for normal transactions.

- Green = High (66-100%) trust. Relax. Safe for all transactions.

Just hold that little Acme Trustometer up and see what part of the display lights up. If it is all green you may be with a group of long-time friends. If only the yellow part of the display lights, trust is conditional. You may be ordering a sandwich and fries at McDonald's. If only the red part of the display lights up, you are either in a very low trust group or there is a stranger at your door trying to sell you a weight loss pill that will change your life for only $109.95.

My experience with many groups over the years leads me to believe that an observant person can make a pretty good guess at the overall trust level in a group. As a workshop facilitator I often set up the meeting room in the thirty minutes before the workshop starts. Participants wander in. They usually come in ones or twos and sit with a friend. As more people file in, the room goes one of two ways. Either the room stays quiet, with just a few folks talking with the person next to them, or the energy continues to rise as people greet each other and get caught up on the news from everyone else.

Energy in a room seems easy to read if you look for it. The amount of positive energy in the room is somehow related to the amount of trust in the group.

Since I can't back this conclusion up with a reading on the Acme Trustometer, you can take it for what it is worth. Begin to notice the groups you are in. Be an outside observer, even as you are an inside participant. Check out the energy. Rate the trust on a percentage scale from zero to 100%: give it a number.

Low Trust International

How else can you measure the level of trust? When I ask people to *"take an imaginary walk in a company with low trust"* and tell me what they see, the responses are remarkably similar. They usually include comments like:

"People are subdued. There is not a lot of energy in the halls. Everything is documented by a memo on the right kind of form. Meetings are polite but a lot does not get discussed. The real issues come out after the meeting in small groups around the water cooler. There are a lot of procedures and rules about what employees can and can't do. There are cliques and factions. People are fearful and act to protect themselves. There are no risks taken. Departments are reluctant to go the second mile for another department."

If you have gone through security check at any airport recently, you know what a low trust environment looks like.

High Trust City

The answers to *"What does a company with high trust look like"* are also predictably similar. People take ownership for what needs to be done. A lot gets done informally, without a lot of forms and paperwork. There is a low level of fear, with free and open communication. I am sure you can fill in your own answers. If you have a higher Aesthetic value you can even tell me the different colors you see in the low trust and high trust environments: a cultural aura.

We can measure trust with the senses that humans have developed over thousands of years. Most of us know when it is there and when it is not.

I had the pleasure of working with a group of people who had built an extremely high trust environment. It had taken time and work to get there. As they were preparing their budget for the coming year and trying to find where to be more efficient, they looked at their single largest expense line item: salary. Due to the nature of the work, which ebbed and flowed unpredictably from day to day, they had a lot of expense in overtime salaries. They often had to ask extra workers to come in, to make sure they had coverage in case of a sudden increase in work orders.

They wanted to reduce their overtime salary cost while maintaining or improving the quality of their service. They had a very aggressive turnaround time goal from orders in to parts out. They hit upon an idea that some people thought was ridiculous and others merely foolhardy. In retrospect it was genius.

The management team decided to let the workers schedule their own overtime. The workers knew best who could come in on a moment's notice and who needed to be at a son's soccer game. The people processing the orders knew best how much overtime was needed and for how long.

It was like operating with a laser instead of a scalpel. At the end of that year they shipped more parts than the previous year, with as good or better turnaround time numbers, for 25% lower overall labor costs.

So What?

The Page asserts that a higher-trust working environment creates better short- and long-term results than a lower trust environment and that competition within an organization creates loss. Better results and less waste imply more efficiency. And yet, much of this work on relationships and reducing competition seems very inefficient. Wouldn't it be simpler to just crack the whip and tell people what to do? We know that gets results. But cracking the whip would never get the results in the overtime example.

Managers are dealing with people, not things; free-will choosing, divergent-problem creating people. Be efficient with the processes, the things. Be effective with people. That effectiveness will, in the long run, yield a more efficient system. The relationships create the results. Trust is the lubricant for the human machine.

A higher trust culture allows for a more empowered, to use an overworked word, place to work. That is, people are willing to risk being more involved in their work. In a higher trust culture people share information and help each other, since information hoarding is not necessary for personal protection. In a higher trust culture the level of cooperation allows real teamwork to exist. There is no need to create a CYA e-mail trail for every risk you take. Authority to act is delegated deeper into the organization — like deciding on who works overtime for how long — because people are trusted to do the work they know how to do and make the decisions they know how to make.

In a higher trust culture there is consistency between word and deed. Managers are said to "walk their talk." Departments are more willing to work through disagreements with a win-win intention, knowing that they are connected and interdependent. Both people's actions and the flow of work are more predictable. Interdependence underpins a willingness to change and adapt to respond to changes in the outside world, because the real competitors are "out there," not in the next department.

I said higher trust creates better results than lower trust. I did not say that all we need is trust (or love, to quote The Beatles) and we will succeed. Of course there is more to it than that. However, all else being equal, when you act to raise the trust within a group you have taken a step toward improved results.

In interdependent organizations, trust and competition are tightly coupled and inversely related. That is, as trust increases internal competition decreases. I am not saying one causes the other. I see them in a loop with each other and influenced by other variables. Each can be either a cause or an effect. Of course this virtuous cycle can become a vicious cycle. For example, put a policy in place that increases internal competition. This will have a lowering effect on trust, which further increases competition.

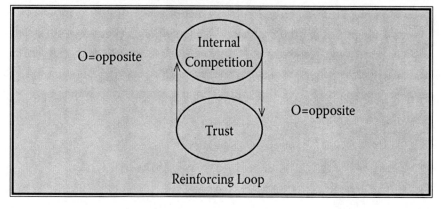

Let's say we've got three shifts working to build Acme Trustometers. Demand is high for this item since a certain book got published. We are a forward thinking company, interested in our people — our most important resource — and also in getting stinking rich.

The executive team decides to offer a little incentive to the teams (to create a little friendly competition) by providing a ten-percent salary bonus to the team with the highest average number of defect-free trustometers produced per shift over the next month. That should get them working harder. Of course, the executives remind the teams about Acme's corporate value of Teamwork and be sure to continue to help each other get better as we learn how to make these things. Which of these two conflicting statements are the teams going to hear?

Yes, Randy, you say, but that kind of thing never happens in real life. Baloney. That kind of thing happens every day, created by well-meaning people. It is just harder to see when it happens in your own culture.

"Oh, good, a contest. Let's whip those idiots on second shift."

ARE WE HAVING FUN YET?

We haven't talked much about how fun varies with trust and competition. My experience says it is more fun to work in a high-trust environment where the competition is directed outward, not within. We would need to get out the Acme Funometer to check for the FQ — the Fun Quotient. And, with production lagging at Acme on the Trustometer, we are not going to get one of those anytime soon.

I was working with a client to define a new position that they were going to create. We used a process that let the job talk so it could tell us what behaviors, motivators and talents were required in this job for superior performance. This information, added to the rest of the hiring process, dramatically increased the odds of finding the best person for that particular job.

I asked one of the participants in this job definition process what the job offered in the way of motivation. *"Why would someone want to do this job?"* I asked. The immediate and sincere answer was, *"The person gets to work in this culture. People love working here."* Maybe fun is a competitive advantage.

NOW WHAT?

1. Consider the trust level where you work. Focus on your part of the organization — your department or area. Rate it on a scale of 1-10, 10 being highest.

    If it is under a seven rating consider what the soft and hard costs are for the people who work there as well as the organization.

    Begin doing one thing to raise the trust. If, heaven forbid, you can't think of anything, then ask your co-workers to help you think of one thing you could do to increase the trust level where you work.

2. Who do people really compete with in your department or organization? Are the people being competed with interdependent or independent of your department or organization? Is it helping or hurting results? What can you do about it?

3. What will your page say about trust and competition?

WIN AS MUCH AS YOU CAN — SCORECARD

Round	A B C D	A	B	C	D	A B C D	A	B	C	D
	The Game Less Often Played					A "Normal" Game				
1	X Y Y Y	+3	-1	-1	-1	X Y Y Y	+3	-1	-1	-1
2	X X X Y	+4	0	0	-4	X X X Y	+4	0	0	-4
3	X X X X	+3	-1	-1	-5	X X X Y	+3	-1	-1	-5
4	X X X X	+2	-2	-2	-6	X X X X	+2	-2	-2	-6
5 (X3)	Y Y Y Y	+5	+1	+1	-3	X X X X	+11	-5	-5	-9
6	Y Y Y Y	+6	+2	+2	-2	X X X X	+12	-4	-4	-12
7	Y Y Y Y	+7	+3	+3	-1	X Y Y Y	+13	-3	-3	-15
8 (X5)	Y Y Y Y	+12	+8	+8	+4	X X X Y	+8	-8	-8	-20
9	Y Y Y Y	+13	+9	+9	+5	X X X X	+7	-9	-9	-21
10 (x10)	Y Y Y Y	+23	+19	+19	+15	X X X X	-3	-19	-19	-31
		+78	+38	+38	+2		+60	-52	-52	-124

THE PAGE

Our work with clients is based on the following assumptions. Everyone does not hold these beliefs. We list them so people we work with will know what to expect from us.

ABOUT INDIVIDUALS:

* Each individual is unique. He or she values ideas, things and people differently and responds to challenges differently. When individuals work together these differences can create chaos or synergy.
* People choose their behavioral responses to what happens to them and are therefore responsible for their own behavior. They choose the best behavior they can think of based on internal and external motivation and their abilities. This behavior may or may not be effective.
* Most people want to do well and succeed. They should have control over how they do their work, and understand why they do their work.
* Leadership resides in every person. It is not reserved just for executives and managers.

ABOUT THE CULTURE:

* A high-trust working environment will create better short and long-term results than a low-trust working environment.
* *People need feedback from processes, customers, suppliers and employees of an organization so they can improve. Facts, data and the scientific method provide feedback. Judgment and blame are not feedback.*
* An organization is an interdependent system. Competiti   ithin a culture creates winners and losers, artificial scarcity and loss. It does n   the organization. Competition between independent o

ABOUT ORGANIZATIONS:

* Every organization is perfectly designe   e of over 85% of the problems experienced   gies, structure, policies, procedures, etc. an
* Organizations and individuals grow   care of and improve the assets and resources that create the results desired by the stakeholders.
* An organization stays in existence because all stakeholders, including customers, suppliers, employees, owners and the community are willing and able to continue the relationship.

> *People need feedback from processes, customers, suppliers and employees of an organization so they can improve. Facts, data and the scientific method provide feedback. Judgment and blame are not feedback.*

FEEDBACK AND COMMUNICATION

CHAPTER 6

THE PAGE

People need feedback from processes, customers, suppliers and employees of an organization so they can improve. Facts, data and the scientific method provide feedback. Judgment and blame are not feedback.

WHERE ARE WE?

Imagine that you're going to Bermuda for a well-earned vacation. You've got your hotel picked out and friends have recommended good places to eat. Everything is falling into place. Then you get a note from your air carrier. You decided to save a few bucks and fly that new carrier, Didwe Air. They inform you that they are going to try a new method for more economical air travel. They have decided to do away with not only the food and customer service, but also the expense of normal navigation equipment.

They are going to pay the pilot a bonus if he gets to the island. Think of the savings! There will be none of that wasteful checking with the ground during the flight to see where the plane is. Just fly on. After all, he has flown there before.

A little far fetched, you say? I hope so. When I am flying somewhere I want the pilot to receive all the information he can, as soon as it is available, to improve the odds of a successful flight. Minute-by-minute feedback ensures that the plane does not veer off-course as we head toward that little island in the middle of the Atlantic.

People in organizations — not just pilots — need feedback. But what do we mean by that?

CLOSING THE LOOP

I first heard the term feedback in engineering school. Feedback was a noun. It was part of the signal from the output of a circuit that was "fed back" into a circuit so the circuit could adjust itself to keep its output at the correct level. We called that a closed loop circuit. The output — fed back to the input — closed the loop.

Closed-loop electrical systems are a common part of everyday life. A room thermostat is one common example. It regulates a heating and air conditioning system based on room temperature (the feedback).

True closed-loop feedback has four important characteristics:

1. Unbiased data (the thermostat is accurate),
2. In the moment, or close in time, (the thermostat constantly measures the room temperature),
3. Occurring close to where the adjustment needs to take place (the thermostat is located in the room) so that,
4. The system self-corrects in a seamless manner. (We seldom notice the furnace and air conditioning in a modern house, unless it malfunctions).

These characteristics apply to most well-functioning feedback systems. We only notice them when they malfunction. Think of the last time you heard a squeal from the loudspeaker when someone grabbed the microphone at the local Rotary fish fry. *"I'd like to thank .. SQUUEEEAALLLLL... oops, sorry, all the Rotarians for their time and effort... ."* That system isn't working right and we all know it.

A closed-loop system adjusts itself in the moment to create a desired result based on current relevant data. An open-loop system is running, usually amok, without feedback. The pilot for Didwe Air was going to fly open loop.

ORGANIZATIONAL FEEDBACK

Now apply this feedback concept to organizational life. I think it is safe to state that feedback of some kind is necessary in order for most organizations to be effective. Nothing with much complexity is created without making changes and corrections along the way — closing the loop. The question then becomes: how do we do it?

Organizational feedback that nurtures individuals and propels the organization forward is an element of the culture. It resides in the beliefs, behaviors and conversations of those in the organization. Many organizations try to make feedback a systemic issue rather than a cultural issue. Of course the systems affect the culture. They are both parts of an interdependent system. However, if an organization relies on an annual appraisal system as the main vehicle for feedback, it won't be feedback in our sense of the word because it does not meet the four conditions of our criteria. I would call most annual appraisal systems judgment, not feedback.

In other words, an appraisal system does not use unbiased data, given close to the action and in the moment so that workers can self-correct. It uses subjective conclusions from a human rater — often someone not closely involved with the work — given at the end of the appraisal period — and often connected to a salary distribution system. For feedback to be real and effective, it cannot be relegated to a system.

THE TRANSISTOR HAS NO CHOICE

Electrical circuits have known parameters and variation. In a circuit, if a known input is applied we get a predictable output. People and organizations are not so simple or predictable. Remember our previous discussion of the human as a divergent element? In an organization the conversations about performance are between free-willed humans. Who knows what might happen? Some people conclude that it is just easier to create a system to handle all those messy conversations.

The art of giving and receiving feedback in an organization is a much more divergent problem than the science of creating a closed-loop electronics circuit.

Remember we said that we don't solve divergent problems, because they don't have only one correct answer. We live with them or deal with them as best we can. To do that requires a deep understanding of the problem coupled with a willingness to balance the opposite sides of an apparent paradox.

In this case of organizational feedback one apparent paradox is maintaining control from the top and taking directions from below: balancing tops down and bottoms up. Referring to the four characteristics for true feedback, I might ask,

"How can we provide as much unbiased timely data as possible directly to those doing the work (bottoms up) while maintaining the overall direction for the organization (tops down)?"

This divergent question makes us think about the kind of true feedback needed in organizations.

THE CASE FOR TOPS DOWN

As I watch the news and observe our world, I am struck by the best and worst in human behavior. When lives are turned upside down by a disaster, strangers often pitch in to help. Examples of the worst of human behavior can also be found every night on the evening newscast.

There is good and there is evil. Hartman might say evil exists when people value ideas systemically more than humans intrinsically. Some of you may be thinking, yes, we have some of those people in my organization. Maybe we don't have evil people here — well there is this one guy — but it seems like we do have some people who are more concerned with what they can get away with than how to help their fellow workers. So without some tops down direction (and control) this place would dissolve into anarchy. You are convinced that we need these organizational laws, enforced by control systems.

If an organization is founded on McGregor's Theory X beliefs that we explored in Chapter Four, the appraisal system becomes a logical way to keep tops down control. It can do that, but the unintended side effects include reduced trust, increased internal competition and more energy and time spent figuring out how to get a better rating number than on doing high quality work.

So if we could wave our magic wand, we would create a culture that had plenty of feedback, with everyone focused on a purpose or mission, without the negative side effects.

CULTURAL REPAIR

Emile Durkheim (1858-1917), a Frenchman known as the Father of Sociology, said: *"When mores are sufficient laws are unnecessary; when mores are insufficient, laws are unenforceable."* This quote applies to an organization's rules of the road; the way people treat each other. The mores are in the culture.

The culture in an organization is not static. It grows and changes, gets better or gets worse. Culture is nurtured by managers and supervisors. Workers work in the culture; managers work on the culture. In a culture of mistrust and competition where the mores are insufficient, the job of managers becomes that of parent and security guard. A goal of most organizations should be to create cultures where fewer laws are needed because the people are trusted to look out for themselves, each other and the organization. The old mantra for managers was plan, organize and control. The new mantra is coach, help and try to not get in the way of progress.

In some organizations high control has been the standard operating procedure for a long time. It will take time and effort to rebalance the control versus freedom, or tops down / bottoms up equation in these organizations. To change the culture for the better, we start with the present culture and gradually improve it.

I believe it is possible to intentionally grow a culture of trust, low internal competition and lavish feedback. And I believe it is possible to select people who will, for the most part, respect and grow that culture. In that kind of environment the mores become sufficient and control systems are used in a supporting role. These changes usually take buy-in and support from the top. On the other hand, the story of Gandhi in India or freedom fighters around the world are stories of culture change created by a small critical mass of people who were at odds with the culture of the status quo.

APPRAISE ALL YOUR FRIENDS

As we think about feedback and about freedom and control, recall groups you've been in. Do any display what we could call a feedback culture without a formal system of control?

One place to look is where people get together to accomplish something: maybe it's that Rotary fish fry with the squawking microphone. In my community, companies sponsor United Way Care Days where employees volunteer a day to fix up one of the nonprofit agencies. Other examples include companies with self-managed teams and partnerships operating as self-managed units.

Yet another example is a well-functioning marriage. Its success depends in part on giving and getting feedback, in the moment, in a spirit of authenticity and love.

Would your spouse like an annual written appraisal? (Make sure to give a numerical rating to each individual key responsibility as well as an overall number.)

"Well, honey, looking overall at this last year I rated you a two on cooking and you were above requirements for most of the year on cleaning, but you slipped a little this last quarter, so that is where the three comes from. That's a meets requirements, so it's still pretty good, huh? Can you just sign here on the last page? Hey — where are you going?"

In relationships and organizations where communication and trust and real feedback exist, formal appraisals are unnecessary, even ludicrous.

CONDITIONS FOR A FEEDBACK CULTURE

If we look at some of these examples — the community volunteers, the small business, the well-functioning marriage — and ask what makes them work, we see several common characteristics:

- The people understand their mission and purpose;
- The people share a clear idea of what each person will contribute to the mission — what they will do;
- The people work in a way that fits who they are; for the most part they can be themselves, without having to play a role;
- The people take responsibility for their own work;
- The people take some ownership for the success of the project;
- There is a reasonable level of trust in the relationships of those involved; and
- The people are engaged in developing / building / growing / accomplishing something.

These characteristics are the subjects of the previous chapters of this book. They are important to The Page because they are the building blocks of an effective organization. If an organization's culture does not contain these elements, they are a good place to begin the cultural repair.

CATCH 22

As we think about feedback being given by managers in an organization you may see a Catch 22. Managers are humans. (Yes, they are). All humans are biased by their mental filters. Therefore, you'll protest that humans can't give feedback as I have defined it because feedback comes from unbiased facts and data.

A WAY OUT

Hmm. What to do? I have two suggestions for managers: (1) let the process speak and (2) use a coaching approach to give feedback.

ALL WORK IS A PROCESS

Instead of measuring people and attaching judgmental language to their accomplishments, measure the work processes and look for improvements.

All work is a process. A process, very simply, is the steps we go through to complete some task. The work that we do is, to an extent, repetitive. Our work can be improved upon as we observe what we are doing this time and make improvements to how we do it — process improvement — the next time. Some people prefer to see work as a series of unconnected random events that show up on their desk. There is some uniqueness to our work each time we perform it — variation, if you will. But much of the variation is predictable and controllable within limits. This is called common variation.

Some people also say, *"Just let me do my work and leave me alone. I don't need to know what anyone else is doing."* That would be nice, but few organizations work that way. Just like in the Win As Much As You Can game in the last chapter, what one person does affects others. Most work is not independent. The cry "Let me do my thing" is a wish for a simple world that does not exist in organizations.

If we consider work as a combination of related processes that come together to become larger, more integrated systems, then we can begin to envision how an organization operates. Next let's see how we can get true feedback from these processes. Consider the one block process diagram below.

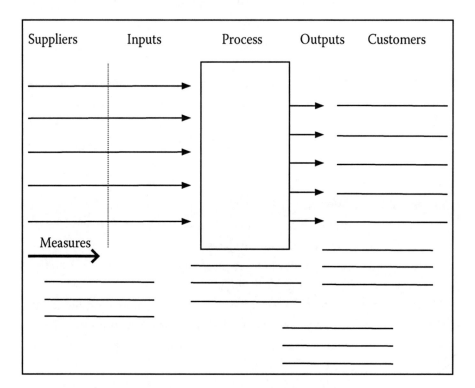

This is a generic way to look at any process. In this simple diagram, whatever process we want to examine is shown as the one block in the middle. This diagram helps us understand where the process begins and ends and how it interacts with other processes to create a larger system. If you have been using process diagrams in your organization, this will seem simple to you. The concept of seeing work as a process and identifying the feedback within that process is what I want to communicate.

If you have been mapping and improving your processes and reducing the variation in those processes for years, as is being done in many organizations, feel free to skip this part or send me your suggestions for improvements.

For example, let's look at the process of producing a quarterly report. Every process has suppliers who give us the information and other resources we need to run the process. The suppliers in the quarterly report process are the people who send in the required data toward the end of the quarter. Another supplier could be the people who maintain the computers where the data is kept and transferred.

The inputs are the data, for example, our revenue from sales. Other inputs could include the computers needed to complete the report.

The output is the report. Customers are anyone who receives and uses the report.

The process of writing the report is itself a series of activities performed in a certain sequence. In this quarterly report example it might include collecting the data, inputting data to an Excel spreadsheet, applying certain factors, sorting the new data into various categories, saving the report in the proper place and sending the finished document to the proper distribution list.

Listen To The Work

The purpose of the quarterly report process is to provide a report to the correct customers in an accurate, readable format, on the given date. The quarterly report will be produced correctly if and only if all the process steps are completed correctly, using correct inputs.

We can measure these expectations, to see if the report is produced on-time and defect free and, if not, where to look to improve the process. Our one block diagram contains a place for measures of the input, the process itself, the outputs and the customers' feedback. These measures, when compared against a standard of what should be and what could be, create both the feedback needed to keep the process on course and provide information about where the process could be improved.

Some of the measurements come from humans. Feedback is their view of reality about the process. However, it is not directed specifically at another human. It is their view of how well the process is presently fulfilling its purpose. To the extent possible, objective, rather than subjective, measures are chosen for feedback. For instance, a measure of the output — the report itself — could be whether or not the report is in every customer's e-mail by close of business on the last work day of the month.

How could we measure the <u>input</u> data? Asking *"Is the information we received complete, accurate and on-time?"* is one approach.

What measures would be relevant for the <u>process</u> itself? We could measure the amount of effort and resource needed to complete the report. We could measure the turnaround time — how long it takes from start to finish.

One of my client's Accounting Department tracks how many days after the end of the month it takes them to close the books. They are working to shorten this time while maintaining or improving the quality of the data provided. We could also measure how the people who produce the quarterly report are improving their capacity and capability through training or other means.

What about <u>customer</u> measures? With my clients I often use the simple but effective "Continue, Stop, Start." For example:

1. What was most useful about this report that you want and need us to <u>continue</u> providing to you?
2. What about this report is not useful for you? (<u>stop</u>)
3. What is missing from this report that you would like to see added? (<u>start</u>)

Process diagrams are an effective way to measure and improve processes without judgment and blame.

NOT A NEW IDEA

The idea of improving work by studying processes is not new. On page 100 is a diagram similar to what Dr. Deming first drew for the top managers of Japanese industry when he lectured there in August 1950. Deming made the point that they should treat their manufacturing plants as systems, receiving feedback from customers to improve the products produced, the processes used and the supplies and parts from vendors.

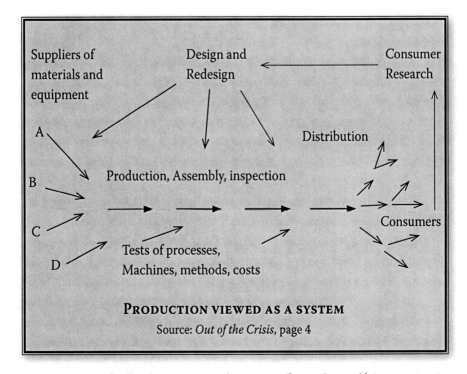

PRODUCTION VIEWED AS A SYSTEM
Source: *Out of the Crisis*, page 4

Receiving feedback is necessary but not sufficient by itself. In our circuit analogy, if the connection between the feedback and the circuit itself is broken, the feedback information cannot get through to serve its purpose of providing corrective information. The circuit will, as we said earlier, run open loop.

Similarly, in our example above, if the feedback is not used to improve the quarterly report process and output, that process is no better off than one that collects no feedback.

I mention this because I have seen and at times been a part of, processes where data were collected and beautifully displayed, but not used to improve the process. How could this happen, you wonder?

SICK SIGMA

Let's say that a company wins a prestigious prize like the Malcolm Baldrige National Quality Award, established by Congress in 1987 to help improve quality in American businesses. The president of another company, wanting to improve, reads an article about the award-winners. The article says they used Six Sigma to improve their processes. The president decides, *"We'll use Sick Sigma to improve our processes, too."*

They create a department with a catchy name to *drive* this change. Next a memo goes out from the newly-created position of Chief Sigma Officer (CSO), stating that each department must have its Five Key Measures (FKMs) displayed prominently in the hall within a week. The status of the displayed measures will be the first topic discussed at the monthly officers' meeting.

Next week everyone has little charts up on the wall. Marketing's charts are in color. The Sales Department makes up some numbers for their charts. The Engineering charts have upper and lower control limits and two decimal places. The Training Department hires somebody to teach chart making. Everyone is required to attend the Six Sigma training. Earn your purple belt here. Get your T-shirt.

A couple months later you visit this organization. You see a chart on the wall and you notice that the little line goes up and down. You ask someone what it means. He looks at it for a while and says, *"Well, some days are better than others."*

My intent is not to be disrespectful of Six Sigma. It is a methodology based on sound statistics that focuses organizations on their defects and opportunities for improvement. It has been the catalyst for improving some organizations. For example, Motorola used it with great success to help them win a Baldrige Award. Because it is a methodology based on statistics it appeals to an engineering culture, such as Motorola. But if that same methodology is imported into a culture not grounded in statistics and data, it may become less than helpful. In fact, it may be virtually useless there. For example, the June 11, 2007 issue of *Business Week* featured a cover story about how 3M tried to use Six Sigma. The cover reads, "3M's Innovation Crisis — How Six Sigma Almost Smothered Its Idea Culture."

I have worked in an organization that mandated six sigma charts, without preparing the necessary foundation for them. A lot of time was wasted generating charts that were not connected to any system improvements.

That is one way an organization can collect feedback but not use feedback. Our organization did not have the beliefs, structures and philosophies that went with a data-driven culture. So we collected data as instructed, but only to satisfy people above, not for improvement.

LOSE THAT UGLY FAT FAST!

The larger point here is not about Six Sigma. It is about trying to import something, anything, into a culture that is not consistent with the culture.

Installing teams in an organization without the necessary training, support and acceptance at all levels is another example. These are the organizational equivalents to the latest fad diets that promise huge weight loss in a short amount of time with no effort. I've heard it referred to as MBBS: Management By Best Seller.

At best there are short-term gains, at worst there is increased cynicism as one more fad floats in on the wings of good intentions and then is rejected as a foreign body by the organization's immune system.

Let's put on our Four Levels glasses from Chapter 1 to examine what's really happening in these situations. Having visible measurements is generally regarded as a good thing. They can become, however, just a <u>behavior</u> brought into a particular company unless it is sustained by that company's <u>structures</u> and, more importantly, consistent with its <u>beliefs</u> and philosophies. If these connections are not made this initiative, as well as any other similar one, will die from lack of life-giving organizational support.

This is not about whether to put up measurements on the wall. In general, having visible, relevant measures about our work is helpful. But, do not put up measures if they are not relevant, or if the groundwork has not been laid so that people will use the measures to improve.

Having measures is not the goal. Being an organization that uses in-the-moment feedback is the goal.

To Have or To Be

What we have — such as measurements on the walls — must proceed from what we are, or it will be useless. I had this having or being idea explained to me by Bob Burdick at IBM years ago. I clearly remember sitting in a conference room, just the two of us, as he walked me through the logic. It hit me like a ton of bricks. It was another paradigm shift for me.

Bob said that in many organizations and in many lives, the priority of things goes from Have → Do → Be. We start with the *Have*. For instance, in the above example, if we can just *Have* Six Sigma in our company, we can *Do* those charts and we will *Be* successful.

It starts by needing something we don't have, so we can create what we want. In other words, the solution, the technology, the consultant, the savior is out there.

Rich Ends From Simple Means

Bob pointed out exceptions to this pattern. For example, some people seem to *have* everything they need but are still unhappy or unsuccessful; other people *have* very little but create much from it. Therefore, he suggested, perhaps the Have → Do → Be route does not explain success. Then he suggested a different approach.

The Leadership approach flows this way: Be → Do → Have.

Everything we do and have stems from who we are. Who <u>are</u> we? We are a world-class electronics manufacturer. Then, what do we <u>do</u>? We apply statistics to our processes because that is the way a world-class electronics manufacturer measures itself. It makes sense to us. What will this kind of rigorous process control and improvement create? We believe it will create the highest quality products produced with less waste ... and maybe a Baldrige award. We will <u>have</u> high-quality products as a result of who we are.

Let me be clear. I am not saying we should not create goals and measures, or haves. I am not saying we can reach our goals without tools and methods and doing. The master carpenter needs plans and carpentry tools.

I am talking about the order of things. Which way does cause and effect flow? If the person is not a master carpenter, or on his way to becoming one, the best plans and the sharpest tools will not yield fine furniture.

The *Be* resides inside each of us. We each decide for ourselves — with influences from others — who we are and who we are becoming. It is one of the stories we tell ourselves.

Every organization also decides who it is. It does things consistent with its identity: who it is. This belief drives the organization's natural behavior and is at the heart of its culture.

Leadership does not start with the *Have*. The *Have* is the desired result. In our Four Levels language the result, the *Have*, is Level 1. Level 1 flows from Levels 2 and 3: behaviors and structures — things we *Do*. And, those levels are preceded by Level 4, beliefs and ideas — or what we can *Be*.

These Have, Do and Be terms relate in a circular way, not just in a linear way. That is, the cause creates the effect and the effect then connects back and influences the cause.

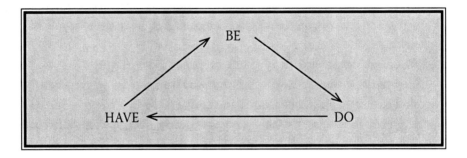

Because this chapter is about feedback, if we add one more element to this diagram it may make more sense. Feedback consists of the facts and data about how we are progressing on our way to the goal. It tells us if we are on target.

We said having data without doing something with it was useless. So, when we have data, checking it right there, tells us if we are getting closer to the planned target: toward what we wanted to "Be."

LIGHTS, CAMERA, ACTION

Actually, we need to do more than Check or Study the data. We need to also take action based on the data — here is where we adjust or modify the next cycle of the loop.

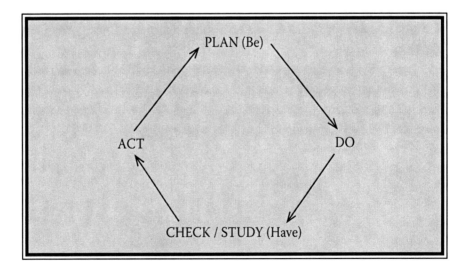

- If we are we getting the results we expected: keep going;

- If we are we headed in the wrong direction: change something; AND

- If we are going for the wrong results: stop;

- When you find yourself in a hole, stop digging. If you shoot yourself in the foot, don't reload.

PDCA Cycle

We have backed into the Plan Do Check Act (PDCA) cycle, or Deming Cycle, as the Japanese businessmen referred to it after Dr. Deming taught it to them in the summer of 1950. Deming called it the Shewhart cycle because he had learned it from his mentor, Walter Shewhart at Bell Labs. The PDCA cycle is much older than Deming or Shewhart. It is in the genetics of every living system that evolves to survive. It is nature's feedback. It is also a succinct way of explaining what may be called the scientific method.

The first step in the cycle says, create a mental construct of what is to be accomplished (plan). Next perform a trial or experiment (do). Study the results to see if the results match the plan (check). Based on the results, take action to change the plan (act). Then expand the experiment if it appears on track, or abandon the experiment if is way off base.

If we are looking at a process that is up and running, we would start with the Check. Study the current results. Are they getting us what we want? Are we getting any unintended side effects that we don't want? What should we try next?

When you use the PDCA process notice the feel of curiosity, learning and experimenting that accompanies it — as opposed to assigning blame and punishing someone.

This cycle is a tool for a learning culture that asks, *"What went wrong in the process?"* The blame culture asks, *"Who screwed up?"* To check a process or decision implies a non-judgmental mindset. The process is seen as an interesting experiment with data and feedback to be studied.

How often is a decision made or action taken and no one really checks up on the outcomes? The assumption is, *"It will work as planned."* There is only a brief Plan followed by Do — another example of operating open-loop. Some people might say that is why there is so much do-do in our organizations.

Checking a process or decision often leads to one or more of the following conclusions:

- We were not clear about our objectives;
- People in the group began with different objectives (did you say dog?);
- We were not clear about our methods; and
- We had unrealistic expectations.

Check often reinforces the need for more Plan. In other words, Check tells us we started with an unclear plan. Two questions often overlooked during initial planning are:

- What do we want to change; and
- How will we know change is improvement?

If we are a culture of learning and improvement, then Plan — Do — Check — Act is a way of thinking and becomes a part of what we do: every decision, action and process.

Coaching As Feedback

Examining processes is one way of getting true feedback. Organizations are made up of the work and the humans who do the work. The process approach looks at the work. Coaching looks at the humans.

I have used the skills of coaching in my work for a number of years. I have taught these skills to hundreds of supervisors, managers and others whose job it is to get results interdependently with others. Coaching is relatively easy to learn and then you can spend the rest of your life mastering and improving your coaching skills.

There are a number of approaches to coaching and it is another experiment an organization may try based on a "Have" or a "Be". I can sometimes tell where they are coming from on the basis of my conversation with the client. If I hear something like the following, I get concerned:

"Randy, could you come in here and give our people some coaching training? It would help if you could squeeze it down to a half-day session. We are really busy."

Like the other tools we discussed, coaching works best when it is in sync with the company's culture and systems.

The coaching approach that I learned from Ron and Carol Ernst at Leadership Horizons, in Carmel, Indiana, uses theory developed by Dr. William

Glasser. Glasser calls his approach Choice Theory and Reality Therapy and he has written a number of books on the subject. Glasser first practiced his approach in California mental hospitals in the sixties. The Ernsts have done a masterful job of applying Glasser's clinical theory to the business environment.

I understand that the term "coach" was first used in the U.S. by college students around 1900 who referred to the professors who helped them get through their classes efficiently as coaches — referring to the horse-drawn stagecoaches which were, in their day, the fastest conveyance to get someone from where they were to where they needed to go. This is a good analogy for modern coaching in an organization.

We can use the Plan — Do — Check — Act cycle as the foundation for a coaching conversation. The four basic coaching questions are:

1. **What do you want? (Plan)**

   What do you want to happen? What do you want to create? This is the starting point, to see if what the person being coached wants is in line with the purpose of the organization, the work of the department, reality and other checks. It corresponds to the *Plan* part of the Plan — Do — Check — Act cycle. We ask the question because what someone else wants is not visible to us. It resides in their head and some variant on this basic question makes it visible.

2. **What have you done to get what you want? (Do)**

   As Ron Ernst says, *"You can't think or feel your way to a result. You must do something."* Interestingly enough, people are often much clearer about what they want than what they have done to get what they want. This is the *Do* part of the Plan — Do — Check — Act cycle and this question encourages the person being coached to review his or her actions.

3. **Is what you are doing getting you closer to what you want? (Check)**

   This is the *Check* part of the cycle. It gives the person being coached a chance to self-evaluate their progress. At this stage of the conversation, most managers feel compelled to judge the other person's actions. A manager who says *"I used to have that job. Believe me, what you are doing won't work"* is judging, not coaching. It may or may not be helpful, but it is not coaching.

The coach might say something like, *"Do you think what you are doing now is going to work for you?"* or a thousand variations on that theme. Usually the person being coached knows better than anyone else whether their approach will work. And, if it is their idea, they will work harder to make it work. Then the coach becomes an accountability partner for the person being coached.

Responsibility stays with the person responsible for completion of the work.

If I, as your coach and manager, tell you to do something, you may do it out of compliance or deference to my position. You may not be committed to the idea, or think it is a good idea or want to do it. The coach trades compliance for commitment by encouraging the person being coached to come up with his or her own plan of action. This leads us to the fourth question:

4. **What is your plan? Or, what is your next action? Or, what do you need to do next? (Act)**

    This very important question establishes a feedback of sorts, to start the next coaching conversation. When the person being coached establishes a clear, simple plan of action it means that person can do something to move closer to what he or she wants.

Although the coach may help the person being coached create a plan, the emphasis is on encouraging the person to create his own plan. The person is more likely to own it if he created it. This moves him away from being a victim and puts him more in charge of his life.

Since coaching usually involves a series of conversations (typically once a week), the plan also gives the coach a place to begin the next conversation. The coach can use a variation of the Do question. Did you accomplish your plan? If the answer is yes, that is good, keep coaching the person forward. If the answer is no, then the coach can work with the person to get them back on the right track quickly. A good plan ensures that the problem being dealt with will get resolved. It closes the feedback loop.

THE ART OF COACHING

You can see that these are easy questions to learn. The art is in the way you ask them, the order you ask them, how well you can resist telling the other person what to do and a number of other variables. That is why our basic coaching workshop is two days long and our best coaches have been through the workshop several times. Coaching is a great example of the Army's adage that you haven't learned it until you have done it. With practice and support most people can integrate coaching skills into their management tool box.

I mentioned earlier my distaste for the annual appraisal system. I have helped organizations stop doing appraisals. Coaching is the cultural skill that replaces the appraisal system and keeps those cultures from running open-loop.

So What?

Feedback and measures can be important tools for an organization. Measures disconnected from the work, the culture, the people, or the purpose of the organization are useless and / or harmful.

Measures used as control devices in a culture of high control may be necessary for short-term survival but will not lead to long-term effectiveness. Measures used as a non-judgmental dashboard — in the context of a supportive culture of learning and based on a sense of purpose and mission — are invaluable. Taking a process improvement approach to work, learning and practicing the skills of coaching, are two ways to use measures and give feedback in a helpful manner.

The Nun and the Bureaucrat, written by Louis M. Savary and Clare Crawford-Mason, tells the stories of how several hospitals used measurements to improve themselves. They applied Deming's ideas along with Toyota's approach to problem solving. Their stories are cleverly told using the quotes of the people involved. It is a book full of interesting examples of what we have been talking about. I mention this book because people may think all this talk of process improvement, feedback and Plan — Do — Check — Act applies only to manufacturing companies. Nothing could be further from the truth. That was one myth the hospitals themselves had to overcome.

Chapter 3 of *The Nun and The Bureaucrat* is titled, "The Most Surprising Challenge We Faced: The Lost Patient." The chapter describes how the increasing complexity of health care had gradually caused medical professionals to forget why they were there to begin with. Their analysis led to the conclusion that the entire system had to be refocused on the health and well-being of the patient. That became their purpose or, in our language, the *Be* for the entire system. Once that happened they did different things and did things differently.

"It's very easy for people to get distracted in the issues of finance or in hospital politics or in competition between each other. When we've been able to refocus people on the goal of the whole endeavor — getting the best possible

patient outcomes — people really come together and collaborate to do the best they can to improve patient care. And they share information in the best possible ways." (Page 23).

"That means the staff learns to view their work as scientists who collect data, conceive an improvement and test it. That is called the PDSA cycle: Plan, Do, Study, Act." (Page 92).

The book chronicles their stories. Once the hospital staff clarified their Be, the health and well-being of the patient, they then began to Do the things necessary to ensure patient health and well-being. Their Haves included improvements in patient and employee satisfaction, significant reduction of wasted time and money and most important, reduction of hospital-induced patient infections, suffering and death.

Every organization is unique. Each requires its own answer to the divergent question, "What should we do next?" To find the answer for your organization begin by understanding clearly your own current reality. Next, be clear about what you want your organization to be. Then consider how these time-tested ideas might help you get there.

NOW WHAT?

1. What measures are you using in your own life for feedback?

2. Are they based on who you are?

3. Are they based on data or something else?

4. Do they come from your memory or your imagination?

5. Are they in sync with your purpose?

6. Are they the right measures for who you want to be in the future?
   For example, how do you measure:
   - How you spend your time and energy (time management)?
   - Where the money goes (personal budget)?
   - How you serve others and give back (personal mission)?
   - How you are learning and growing? (personal development plan) your physical health and exercise?
   - What is the right thing to do? (ethics and values)

7. What will your Page say about feedback and communication?

One way to practice Plan — Do — Check — Act is to ask good questions. Start with these. I'm sure you'll think of better ones.

PLAN

What is our mission?
What do we want to create or improve?
What would improvement look like?
How will we measure improvement?
What are the checkpoints, timetable and deadlines?
What resources — time, money, people and things are required?
Who needs to approve this change?
Who else might be affected by this change?
Can we try it on a small scale?

On the subsequent cycles you can review those questions and also ask:
Do we still want the desired outcome?

DO

What is the next step?
What can we do today?
What options or choices do we have?

CHECK

Where are we now?
Are we satisfied?
Are we getting the results we want?
What are the unintended side effects? (Look far and wide for them)
What can we learn from these results?

ACT

What do we want to keep, continue or standardize?
What do we want to stop doing or discard?
What is still missing that we need to start?

Is there more to do on this? If yes, go back to Plan.

Self-Coaching Version of Plan — Do — Check — Act

1. What do I want?

2. What am I doing to get what I want?

3. Is what I'm doing working?

4. What do I need to do next?
   - Will I do it?
   - When will I do it?

.

PART THREE

ORGANIZATIONS

We have completed the first two parts of *The Page*: Individuals and Culture.

In Part One we looked at individuals as unique human beings. In Hartman's terms we looked at them intrinsically. We explored differences in motivations and behaviors. We said that most of them want to contribute and do a good job.

In Part Two we examined the influence of culture on individuals. We explored the practical, extrinsic aspects of culture including cooperation, communication and trust. We concluded that different cultures profoundly influenced individuals' behaviors and therefore created different results.

In Part Three we will look at the non-human parts of the organization such as its systems, structures, policies and procedures. We will explore how these concepts come about and how these systemic aspects of the organization have a huge effect on the culture and the individuals and therefore on results.

Organizations and individuals both depend on a variety of resources to get the results they want. We will take a look at how this plays out in organizational life. Finally we will consider the organization as a part of the other systems it depends on and as a part of the larger systems it exists within.

THE PAGE

Our work with clients is based on the following assumptions. Everyone does not hold these beliefs. We list them so people we work with will know what to expect from us.

ABOUT INDIVIDUALS:

* Each individual is unique. He or she values ideas, things and people differently and responds to challenges differently. When individuals work together these differences can create chaos or synergy.
* People choose their behavioral responses to what happens to them and are therefore responsible for their own behavior. They choose the best behavior they can think of based on internal and external motivation and their abilities. This behavior may or may not be effective.
* Most people want to do well and succeed. They should have control over how they do their work, and understand why they do their work.
* Leadership resides in every person. It is not reserved just for executives and managers.

ABOUT THE CULTURE:

* A high-trust working environment will create better short and long-term results than a low-trust working environment.
* People need feedback from processes, customers, suppliers and employees of an organization so they can improve. Facts, data and the scientific method provide feedback. Judgment and blame are not feedback.
* An organization is an interdependent system. Competition within a culture creates winners and losers, artificial scarcity and loss. It does not help the organization. Competition between independent organizations is acceptable.

ABOUT ORGANIZATIONS:

* *Every organization is perfectly designed to get the results it is getting. The root cause of over 85% of the problems experienced by organizations is found in the systems, strategies, structure, policies, procedures, etc. and NOT directly due to pe*
* Organizations and individuals grow care of and improve the assets and res the stakeholders.
* An organization stays in existence ers, suppliers, employees, owners and t nue the relationship.

> *Every organization is perfectly designed to get the results it is getting. The root cause of over 85% of the problems experienced by organizations is found in the systems, strategies, structure, policies, procedures, etc. and NOT directly due to people.*

ORGANIZATIONS REFLECT THEIR CREATORS' BELIEFS

CHAPTER 7

THE PAGE

Every organization is perfectly designed to get the results it is getting. The root cause of over 85% of the problems experienced by organizations is found in the systems, strategies, structure, policies, procedures, etc. and NOT directly due to people.

BAD NEWS SIR, YOUR FRAMISTAT IS SHOT

A few years ago Sears made the news in a negative way (see *The Fifth Discipline Fieldbook*, pg. 111). Based on consumer complaints to the California Department of Consumer Affairs and the ensuing sting operation, it was discovered customers were being sold auto parts and services that were not needed. In fact, customers were being overcharged by an average of $223 per visit. In the end, Sears was fined heavily and lost customer loyalty.

As the story unfolded it became clear why Sears' employees behaved this way. Sears offered an incentive program that put serious money in the pockets of employees who sold certain items. Why would Sears do that? As the saying goes, it seemed like a good idea at the time. Sears was under tough competition from Wal-Mart and K-Mart and was losing market share. The managers thought that this incentive program would be a foolproof way to get the employees to sell more. Their program worked.

BLAME THE SYSTEM

Deming, Juran and others have taught that the potential to eliminate mistakes in the workplace lies mostly in improving the systems through which work is done, not in blaming individuals.

Deming taught that 85% of a worker's performance is determined by the system he is working in and the other 15% is due to individual effort. This became known as the Deming Rule. As Deming got older he modified this rule to 94% sytems and 6% individuals. In a *Los Angeles Times* interview dated December 5, 1993, Deming said, *"All that happens comes from the system, not the workers. It is absolutely frightening, just frightening."*

Unless Deming is radically mistaken, we should be putting most of our improvement focus on the organization's structure and systems and not on trying to fix the people.

Of course we should hire the best people for the positions we have. We should train and coach people so they have what they need to do their jobs well. In fact hiring, development, coaching, mentoring and retention policies and systems are among the most important in an organization.

The sum of all the systems, policies and procedures, both explicit and implicit, creates the results of the organization. And since the organization was created by and the structure is maintained by the executives and managers, Dr. Deming laid the fault of poor organizational performance at the foot of the managers, not the workers.

QUESTION: WHO SCREWED UP?

Looking at an organization in this way may at first feel counterintuitive. What do you mean it isn't the workers' fault? Who is doing this shoddy work? The immediate natural response to a problem is "Who screwed up?"

Let's look at this situation through our Four Levels glasses. Remember the four levels: the events or results (Level 1) created by the organization are visible. They are today's headlines. As humans it is very hard for us NOT to connect two events in a causal connection. That is, today's result must have been caused by today's person who is doing the job. However, one of the key principles in system thinking is that cause and effect are often separated by space and / or time.

ANSWER: A REASONABLE PERSON

Results do not just show up out of the blue. Today's results are caused by behaviors over time. While it is true that individuals *behave,* a helpful question may be "Why would a reasonable, rational, decent human being do that?" Even if you have a more negative view of the people you work with, it is useful to begin with the assumption that they are reasonable.

Reasonable people behave based on their internal and external motivation, as we discussed in earlier chapters. But in this thing called an organization, external and perhaps internal motivation and behaviors are strongly influenced by structure, which includes all of the systems, policies, procedures and rules both written and unwritten, that govern the system.

In system thinking the structure influences behaviors. Since behaviors create results, structure is an event generator. Therefore, every organization is perfectly designed (Level 3 structures) to get the results (Level 1 events) it is getting. We don't normally blame problems on structure because the structure itself is mostly invisible. The result and the person's behavior are more visible. It is therefore easier to put the blame on a person who is just acting reasonably, given the structure he finds himself in. If you don't like the results, change the organizational design. Even if it's a default design — it's designed.

The fourth level in the Four Levels model is the level of beliefs, paradigms and prejudices — the mental constructs that give our life meaning. We hold these truths to be self-evident. In any organization the self-evident truths held by the people creating the organization result in its structure. To make things more interesting, in most organizations these beliefs are often tacit or unspoken. They are "just the way it is."

Do we believe we can't trust people? If so, we put in a lot of checks and balances. Do we think only managers can make key decisions? Then we put in a lot of hierarchy. Are development engineers more important than manufacturing engineers? Obviously! Make sure development gets the newest computers. Do we think people won't do their best on their own? Maybe we should reward them for selling more auto parts.

To summarize how this pattern looks with our Four Levels glasses on: events (Level 1) are caused by behaviors over time (Level 2). Behaviors over time flow naturally from the structures (Level 3) of the system. The structures were established based on the thinking (Level 4) of the creators of the organization.

OPEN WIDE, SAY AHH

The Four Levels can be used to both diagnose and prescribe. When you see something happening in an organization that does not appear to be serving all the parties, instead of blaming the people involved, or just putting a band-aid on it, look deeper. If your child doesn't feel well you usually don't blame your child (I hope). You or your doctor look for the deeper cause of this ill feeling.

So it is in an organization. Go below the visible behaviors and the structures themselves to the thinking that created the structure. To diagnose, begin at level 1 and work your way to Level 4. Each deeper level will yield a deeper root cause of the event. For example:

Level 1.　<u>Event:</u> A key employee just left.

Level 2.　<u>Behavior over time:</u> This is not a unique event. We have data showing that our turnover rate has been steadily increasing over the past year. The exit interview reports point to problems with our new supervisors.

Level 3a.　<u>Structure:</u> Two years ago HR eliminated the new supervisor training program as a cost savings.

Level 3b.　<u>Structure:</u> Eighteen months ago the company offered a buyout for more experienced supervisors, also to improve our financial position.

Level 4.　<u>Belief:</u> Executives think we can save money by eliminating training and reducing the number of expensive supervisors.

FIXES THAT FAIL

In a Fram oil filter commercial on TV from many years ago, the greasy old mechanic looked into the camera and said, *"Pay me now, or pay me later"* as he was replacing an engine, obviously due to using dirty oil. I'm reminded of that old guy every time I see a shortsighted organizational policy that saves money in the near term and then gives back the alleged savings and more in the long run.

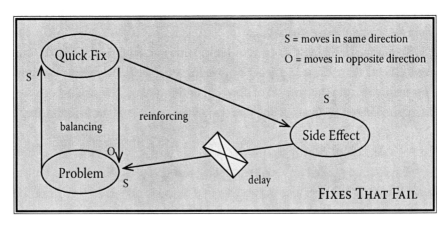

S = moves in same direction
O = moves in opposite direction

FIXES THAT FAIL

This reliance on a short-term fix — a band aid, any port in a storm, a finger in the dike — is so pervasive it has earned the name Fixes That Fail in system thinking circles. When you say, *"That looks like a Fix That Fails"* to a system-thinker, a very specific pattern pops in her head. It looks like the diagram on the previous page.

The diagram shows a problem arising. When it becomes painful enough we take immediate action (quick fix) that, in the short run, seems to reduce the problem. However, after time passes, the short-term solution creates an unintended side effect that in the longer term makes the original problem worse. Some examples of Fixes That Fail include:

1. Problem:
   Running late for a meeting.

   Quick fix:
   Save time by not stopping for gas, although your gas gauge is on EEE.

   Unintended side effect:
   Running out of gas, making you really late for the meeting.

2. Problem:
   Budget overages at an electric utility company.

   Quick Fix:
   Put off trimming the trees over the power lines, lowering labor costs.

   Unintended side effect:
   Ice storm downs branches, power lines and poles, causing much larger labor and material costs.

3. Problem:
   Need more customers.

   Quick fix:
   Offer discounts and rebates to lure new customers.

   Unintended side effect:
   Your present customers, disgusted over this treatment, switch to other suppliers who offer them discounts and rebates, thus lowering your customer base.

You get the picture. With just a brief explanation most people can come up with their own examples, from home or personal experience as well as from organizations. These are universal patterns. In every case there is an asset crucial to getting results — gasoline, power lines, customers — that gets ignored until it becomes a problem.

System thinkers know the key to stopping Fixes That Fail from coming back is to go cold turkey on the quick fix — stop doing it — and look for deeper causes.

Applying this idea to our untrained supervisors, we could prescribe a possible solution by beginning at Level 4 and working upward to Level 1. It would work as follows.

> Level 4: Let's reexamine our thinking. We know we need trained supervisors. Obviously we can't put untrained supervisors on the floor, but we lost our informal trainers in the last buyout and we've cut back on the soft skills training. What should we do?

> Level 3: We need to start a new supervisor curriculum. How can we measure its success?

> Level 2: We should expect turnover rates to improve. Over time, we should lose fewer of our key employees, if we have diagnosed correctly.

Five Whys

There are, of course, other ways to discover the root cause of a visible problem. Toyota has a well-known problem-solving technique called the Five Whys. A person doing the diagnosis asks, *"Why did that happen?"* five times and by then she has usually found the root cause of the problem. The why questions are also a good way to work through the Four Levels. Let the answer to the why take you to the next deeper level. You can see how the Five Whys could apply to this issue.

"We lost another good employee."
> Why did that happen?

"She and her supervisor were not getting along and couldn't get it worked out."
> Why did that happen?

"It isn't really the supervisor's fault. He is brand new and got no training. The only supervisor skills he had were those he learned from his old boss, 'Attila' Smith."

"I thought all new supervisors had to go through training and get mentored by one of our experienced managers. Why didn't that happen?"

"Where have you been? In the last round of 'Everybody do the same thing with 10% less,' they cut out that soft skill training and the mentoring program. And, when the last buy-out/downsizing came around — remember, it happened the week before Christmas — most of our better experienced managers — the ones who had been maintaining the culture — saw the writing on the wall and took what they thought was the best offer they would get. I know we need to be fiscally sound, but we will be paying for this cost savings for years."

The Four Levels and the Five Whys can only live in a culture of learning and experimentation among those who created and maintain the organization. If leaders are not getting the results they expect from the organization, they must be willing to look within at their beliefs and structures. Then these leaders can ask if these beliefs are what now best serve all stakeholders, and if those same beliefs might be generating unintended consequences.

I'm not saying that outside forces are never to blame for poor performance. There is a random nature to the world and every organization is a part of the larger systems of community, competitors, regulators, nations, etc. What I am saying is that too often the last place that leaders look to fix their problems is at Dr. Deming's highest percentage place: within. To use a Stephen Covey quote in an organizational context, *"Anytime you think the problem is 'out there,' that thought is the problem."*

DIP THE SHEEP

Reduced training is sometimes seen as the reason for a failure, but it is not always the problem. A rather common occurrence for me is to have a conversation that goes something like this:

"Randy, this is Frank. I'm having some problems. I need you to come in here and train the X Department." (I love it when the client does both the diagnosis and the prescription, leaving me with only the implementation).

"Okay, glad to. What do you want me to train them to do?" I reply.

"They are supposed to be doing Y and they are not doing it," Frank responds.

"What makes you think it is a training problem?"

(pause) *"What do you mean?"* asks Frank.

"Well, there are a number of reasons why people don't do what we think they ought to be doing, but if they already know how to do it, training them to do it again will just annoy them and cost you money."

"Well, we have put them all through what we call our Skills Boot Camp. They are all SBC certified," says Frank.

"Frank, it sounds like they are already trained. Are they able to do the work? I mean, have you got people who are trying to do things that they are not physically or mentally able to do?"

"No, we are using the hiring process you set up for us," he says.

"Oh, well you undoubtedly have the cream of the crop. That is not the problem. Listen Frank, before we embark on some sheep dipping disguised as training, maybe we ought to see what else might be causing the behavior that is annoying you. Have there been any changes in your reporting structure or your policies recently that might have an effect on this department?"

I will interrupt this dialogue here because you can see where this is going. Typically we do a more rigorous diagnosis of the culture, but surprisingly often Frank will say something like, *"Hmm, well we did downsize 30% without removing any of the work. You don't think that is the problem, do you?"*

When it comes to changing policies and structures, which can be done with the stroke of a pen, the strokers almost never do a simple Plan — Do — Check — Act cycle on the change. The result: more do-do.

Check, Please

Quite a few years ago I was working with people who had been involved in several quality improvement projects. I'm a big fan of involving the people doing the work in its improvement. In this case a lady raised her hand and said, *"How can we reverse these improvement projects?"*

I must admit that was the first time I had been asked that question. *"Why do you want to do that?"* I responded.

She explained that she worked in the tool room where she and others made metal parts. There were always little metal shavings that needed to be swept away from the work surface. A recent improvement project had replaced the standard cloth wipes with paper wipes. The improvement team did the calculations, found they could save money and implemented the change. So far, so good, on the **plan** and **do** part.

However, no one came by to **check** with all the users, including the lady who wanted to reverse this project, because the palms of her hands were all cut up by metal filings that had penetrated the paper wipes. If someone had checked, the team could have come up with other options to get the improvement and eliminate the unwanted side-effects.

You may ask, *"Well, why didn't she speak up?"* My response is: ask her. Perhaps the culture and/or organization did not encourage that. We wouldn't know the answer to that until we did a little diagnosing. Was it because she did not know how to confront a superior? In that case, maybe some dialogue training would help. But what if her supervisor told the department that loyal employees support company initiatives and *"you are either with us or against us?"* Or what if her peers teased the last person who spoke up about an ergonomic problem and he is now known as "Wimpy?" Or what if she and her department get rewarded for the number of successful projects implemented? Or what if . . . fill in your own reasons.

I started that story to make the point that changes are often made at the structural level with the tacit assumption that there will be no unintended consequences at the results level. And that just does not fit with reality.

In a culture of learning, we are eager to see what happens with the new policy. Does it serve all stakeholders? Did it do what we intended? Did it do something else we did not intend? If needed, let's modify it and try again. If that curiosity is not there or if there is a culture of ego and blame, when that new policy or improvement doesn't work out, the result is, *"It's not my fault."*

So What?

Organizations are the physical manifestation of an idea that began in the mind of one or more humans. As an organization takes shape in the physical world the good, the bad and the ugly parts all show up. What is happening in that organization today, for better or worse, began some time back in the mind of the founder.

Improvement happens when those who have a deep understanding of the organization are willing to rethink the present setup and modify it for improvement. Organizational improvement is, after all, an extremely divergent problem. It cannot be approached without first having a deep understanding of the present situation.

As we discussed earlier, in Part 1 (Individuals) of this book, telling your story without including the part you played in creating the result is called victim thinking. Victim thinking removes the blame, but it also removes the possibility that you can improve the problem because the problem is out there.

The same pattern applies at the organizational level. Until we look first to improving the organization instead of blaming the workers, we will continue to work on 6% of the problem and ignore the other 94%.

NOW WHAT?

1. Find ways to practice your organizational awareness coupled with curiosity. Begin to observe the organizations you are familiar with.

2. Think of a problem or an unhelpful routine that is going on in an organization — it could be a business or a church or a civic group.

3. Using your Four Levels glasses, come up with five different reasons why the above problem or routine could be existing in that organization. Do this without blaming anyone. Ask the Five Whys.

4. Can you get to some Level 4 beliefs that could have existed in the minds of those who created the organization, to allow that problem to get started? Assume the creators had good intentions. What could they have been thinking?

5. Ask, "What are we really trying to accomplish with this process? Is it still the right process to use to accomplish the goal?"

6. This exercise will get you looking deeper at the organizational structure and beliefs and will also help you remember that just because you see a result, that does not mean you know why that result took place.

7. Identify a Fix That Fails pattern in your own life. Draw it out.

   • What is the cost of not dealing with this problem?

   • What is the addictive attraction of the quick fix?

   • What could you do differently to go cold turkey and eliminate this recurring problem in your life? Will you do it? When?

8. What will your Page say about how and why organizations get results?

THE PAGE

Our work with clients is based on the following assumptions. Everyone does not hold these beliefs. We list them so people we work with will know what to expect from us.

ABOUT INDIVIDUALS:

• Each individual is unique. He or she values ideas, things and people differently and responds to challenges differently. When individuals work together these differences can create chaos or synergy.

• People choose their behavioral responses to what happens to them and are therefore responsible for their own behavior. They choose the best behavior they can think of based on internal and external motivation and their abilities. This behavior may or may not be effective.

• Most people want to do well and succeed. They should have control over how they do their work, and understand why they do their work.

• Leadership resides in every person. It is not reserved just for executives and managers.

ABOUT THE CULTURE:

• A high-trust working environment will create better short and long-term results than a low-trust working environment.

• People need feedback from processes, customers, suppliers and employees of an organization so they can improve. Facts, data and the scientific method provide feedback. Judgment and blame are not feedback.

• An organization is an interdependen[t]   [cre]ates winners and losers, artificial scarcit[y]   [compensat]ion. Competition between independent o[rganizations]

Organizations and individuals grow and prosper to the extent that they take care of and improve the assets and resources that create the results desired by the stakeholders.

ABOUT ORGANIZATIONS:

• Every organization is perfectly designe[d]   [Becau]se of over 85% of the problems experienced by organizations is foun[d in the] systems, strategies, structure, policies, procedures, etc. and NOT directly due to p[eopl]e.

• *Organizations and individuals grow and prosper to the exte[nt] that they take care of and improve the assets and resources that create the results desired by the stakeholders.*

• An organization stays in existence because all stakeholders, including customers, suppliers, employees, owners and the community are willing and able to continue the relationship.

Maintaining Healthy Organizations

CHAPTER 8

The Page

Organizations and individuals grow and prosper to the extent that they take care of and improve the assets and resources that create the results desired by the stakeholders.

Have You Got My Back?

I was working with a group who had been under the tyranny of a boss who didn't believe in renewing peoples' skills. This man was replaced by a friend of mine whom I respected for both his leadership style and character. Plus, my friend made me laugh a lot, he is a good man.

The people who would be working in his group didn't know him. At his request I began training these people in teamwork and interpersonal communications, helping them to catch up with other areas in the company that had received the same training in years past. The previous manager did not invest in this training because he believed they had too much real work to do.

The company was also undergoing reengineering at the same time with the help of consultants. They tested the various departments to determine each one's readiness to change.

One of the other areas in this company, an area that had consistently invested in training for all levels of employees, scored well. They tested completely ready for change. They were a well-renewed resource for the company.

This group I was working with was also ready for change, but in another way — they were tired of being second-guessed, scapegoated and Theory X'ed. By the way, that management style is one answer to the question, *"What happened to our brainpower?"* The people with the most options leave first.

As we finished one of the training days I said to them, *"If your new boss was here right now and you could be completely open with him, what questions would you ask him?"*

Silence ensued, as they tried to decide what I was up to. I said, *"I'm serious. We have been talking about communicating more openly. One part of that is to be able to check out what you are thinking. What are you thinking?"* With not much more probing they filled two charts with questions for their new boss.

I took the two charts to my friend and said, *"I think it would be neat if you came to the next workshop so you could respond to some of these questions. It would sure beat working on examples that were not real."* He was all for it.

Part of what we were doing was working to rebuild trust. I don't remember the whole conversation between the people and the manager, but I'll always remember one part. Since this group had seen managers come and go, their thinking was, *"Here is one more manager, making a brief stop in the basement of the real world, on the way up the corporate ladder."* The question that followed was, *"How long are you gonna stay here?"* The manager answered, *"I live here. I have land and family here. I plan on staying a long time."*

Next question: *"Will you stand behind us when we are right?"*

Manager's answer: *"Stand behind you when you are right? I'll stand behind you when you are right and when you are wrong."* And then he added, *"But if you are wrong a lot more than you are right, I will be changing my answer to your previous question."* Laughter ensued and some beliefs about the manager began to change.

Is there a better way to convey the interdependence of the situation, the truth that we are all in it together? There is an old adage that says, *"People don't care how much you know, until they know how much you care."* Leaders who have their egos in check and are committed to both the mission and the people involved are themselves a precious resource. In his book, *Good To Great*, Jim Collins refers to these leaders as Level 5 leaders. They can unleash the capability and capacity of others who always have a choice to either invest or withhold their discretionary energy from the organization.

Research shows one of the top reasons people give for leaving an organization is the style and skill of their immediate manager. It is said that people join organizations and leave managers.

Renew The Family

We can't have an effective organization without people whose skills are continually renewed. What else does it take to maintain and improve an organization? Let's look at an organization you are familiar with, such as your family. What does it take to maintain and improve your family? Your list of assets and resources would include the members of your family. It might also include your car and your house and its contents. You could also include your neighbors, friends and civic or church groups. Your family depends on them, if not for survival, at least to help it function normally. You might list the love that exists between family members as a precious resource. You would probably include money, both income and savings. You might also include your town.

You get the idea. There are things your family needs to sustain and improve its existence. Your family is interdependent with its surroundings.

What happens to your family when one or more of these resources starts to become depleted? Your house needs painting, the furnace needs replacing, the car needs an oil change and filter, the yard needs fertilizing, the budget needs tweaked, or you and your spouse need a quiet evening together? You take action to get it fixed. Better yet, you think ahead and try to take care of these problems before they become crises. A big part of our lives is spent maintaining our stuff and our relationships.

Whether the organization is your family or my friend's group, it requires constant renewal to grow and prosper. All resources are finite and nothing lasts forever. Taking time to renew and improve those assets and resources that create the results you desire allows you to create more results. Why is it we forget the obvious truth that the rhythm of life is the cycle of use and renew?

I'm going to suggest a cause for our forgetfulness, illustrated in a quote by Charles Hummel, author and former president of Barrington College in Barrington, Rhode Island:

> *"The vital task rarely must be done today, or even this week. The urgent task calls for instant action. The momentary appeal of these tasks seems irresistible and they devour our energy. But in the light of time's perspective, their deceptive prominence fades. With a sense of loss we recall the vital task we pushed aside. We realize we have become slaves to the tyranny of the urgent."*

I like that phrase "tyranny of the urgent." We have all experienced it: something is demanding our attention <u>right now</u>, like a screaming baby (or a screaming boss). Or maybe it's a looming deadline. In any case, this urgent crisis reprograms our reasoning.

When this reasoning reroute happens it spawns at least two problems: (1) a short-term mentality and (2) a growth forever mentality. Let's take a look at these two common patterns from a system thinking perspective.

I DON'T HAVE TIME TO . . .

In the last chapter I introduced the system thinker's pattern known as Fixes That Fail. It thrives on a short-term mentality. Here is the problem or crisis, demanding immediate attention and we have all these other things to do too, so let's just choose the first option that will give us some relief (quick fix) until we have more time to address it systemically.

I used to work for a manager who, when he caught me doing something in a less than acceptable manner ALWAYS said, *"If you don't have time to do it right, when are you gonna have time to do it over?"* I recently read that in 1957 Nobel Laureate and economist Herbert Simon coined the term "satisfice" — a combination of satisfy and suffice — to describe the typical human decision-making process where we accept the first option that offers an acceptable payoff. So, this is not a new problem, but it is a pervasive one.

SHARPEN THE SAW

The basic approach to deconstructing the Fixes That Fail pattern is to quit relying on the short-term solution and fix the root cause of the problem. Don't let the gas tank get so low. Start earlier so you have more time to get to the meeting on time. Review the budgeting system for both long-term and short-term balance. Treat your present, valuable customers as well or better than the new ones you are luring. It is easy to say, but it is often hard to quit cold turkey, particularly if we have become addicted to the quick fix.

Stephen Covey, in his book *The Seven Habits of Highly Effective People*, makes the point for renewal with the well-known tale of the person who is working hard to saw down a tree, while using an obviously dull saw blade. The root cause, in this case, is the dull blade.

"Why don't you stop and sharpen the saw?" asks the passer-by.
"No time," huffs the worker, *"got to get this tree cut down."*

Maybe the root cause is the dull person wielding the blade. Covey contends that this 7th Habit of "Sharpen The Saw" — the habit of renewal — strengthens all other habits.

Fixing the root cause almost always takes longer, requires more effort or discipline or money and in general is a bitter pill to swallow. If you are dealing with an issue and someone says *"Haven't we fixed this problem before?"* then you are probably about to take another ride on the Fixes-That-Fail merry-go-round. I was explaining this to a group of managers and one said, "What we need is a good, long-term quick fix." Succumbing to the tyranny of the urgent by relying on a quick fix and not addressing the root cause of the problem is one way to not take care of your assets and resources.

IF IT AIN'T BROKE, DON'T FIX IT

The second problem created by the tyranny of the urgent is a "growth forever" mentality. That is, what has been working is surely going to keep working. While we all realize that nothing grows without limit we often act against that knowledge. This is graphically represented by the system thinker's pattern below: Limits to Growth.

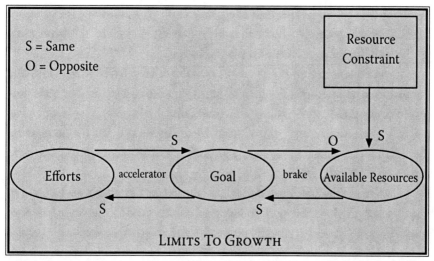

Limits To Growth states that many systems initially grow quickly because they've been invested in and they have plenty of room to grow. For example, let's say we are introducing the Airgo Coupe, a new car that looks like a million bucks and runs on air.

In the diagram above, the Goal is to sell cars. Initially they sell like hotcakes. This moves us closer to our goal, because our Efforts — such as assembling a motivated sales force, advertising in all the best media outlets, and having an impossible technology that kicks fossil fuel's butt — create a customer backlog. This pattern reminds me of when I was on a waiting list for one of the first Miatas to hit the streets.

In this early part of the life cycle the left-hand loop, the accelerator, dominates. This is true for most new efforts, programs, or services. There is initially plenty of room for growth. We read in the paper that some company has doubled in size. Reading the second paragraph we see they have grown from two to four employees.

As sales continue, limited resources such as parts to make the Airgo, are used. Growth continues until the system hits a barrier to growth, called a Resource Constraint in the diagram. In our case the fuelerator that converts air into motion has some manufacturing problems. Our vendor can't make enough to meet the manufacturing commitment. The fuelerator becomes our Resource Constraint.

The fuelerator limits the growth of our system — in this case, sales of the Airgo. Now the right-hand side of the diagram, the brake, dominates. If we continue to focus our efforts on selling more cars by, say, lowering the price, we are just shooting ourselves in the foot and reloading. Actions on the growth side at this point in the cycle are counterproductive.

In systems, accelerators and brakes are sometimes referred to as reinforcing loops and balancing loops. Imagine sitting in your car pushing on the accelerator while your passenger is pulling the emergency brake. Not very productive. At that point, the system (car) is ruled by the brake and not the accelerator. Sometimes the barrier is relatively easy to fix. *"Please release the brakes, dear, we are ready to go."*

Sometimes the barrier is difficult, expensive or has a long lead time. For example, at Airgo we may need to invest in, construct and bring online another manufacturing facility to handle an anticipated increase in the Airgo's future sales demand.

THE LION IS WEARING RUNNING SHOES

The key to postponing the brake part of a Limits To Growth pattern is to anticipate what the next barrier is going to be, such as the need for more manufacturing capacity and to begin working on that before it becomes a Resource Constraint. Checking out the gas gauge and filling up before you hit empty is usually a relatively easy thing to do. Committing capital funds and investing in a high-tech manufacturing facility, well before the finished plant is needed, is a more difficult decision. Both decisions reduce a barrier to getting the desired results.

Nothing grows without limit. Understanding and acting on the next limit to growth is the way out of the second problem generated by the tyranny of the urgent: a growth forever mentality. Anticipating and removing more road-blocks than the competition is one way to stay ahead of the game.

I am reminded of that old joke about two guys out in the jungle. They see a lion and the lion sees them. One guy takes off running. The other one says, *"Don't be silly. We can't outrun that lion."* The other one says, *"I know. I only need to outrun you."*

I guess the runner saw that as an independent situation. It was either him or the other guy. In an interdependent situation they would have worked together to get away from the lion, but the joke wouldn't have been as funny.

WHAT IS THE SCORE?

Renewal is a natural outcome of the Plan — Do — Check — Act cycle. During the Check we ask, *"How is this particular asset holding up?"* During the Act part of the cycle we ask, *"What do we need to do to protect and restore it?"*

I'm typing this draft on a laptop computer. The display tells me that I've got 66% of my battery charge remaining. I recently plugged the computer into the wall outlet so while I'm using it I'm also recharging the battery. In the larger system, I am using the assets of the planet to charge that battery.

It is easy to check the battery in my computer. How would you check the health of organizational assets, especially those that are most important to the success of your organization? If only there was an organizational dashboard to give us feedback on our key assets.

Drs. Robert Kaplan and David Norton have popularized a feedback approach they call The Balanced Scorecard (www.bscol.com). In numerous books and articles they point out that most organizations have all kinds of measuring devices trained on the traditional financial bottom line. In The Balanced Scorecard the authors suggest using four bottom lines to get a more balanced view of key assets. In addition to (1) the financial perspective, they suggest looking at (2) the customer perspective, (3) the internal business perspective and (4) the innovation, learning and growth perspective.

In a 1992 article in *Harvard Business Review* Kaplan and Norton stated that a balanced scorecard provides answers to four basic questions:

- How do customers see us? (customer)

- What must we excel at? (internal business)

- Can we continue to improve and create value? (innovation and learning)

- How do we look to shareholders? (financial)

Using these questions as the starting point for a conversation among the members of the organization is one way to identify key resources and their present condition.

The Balanced Scorecard is a tool. In a previous chapter we looked at ways that tools and techniques can be misused. We used Six Sigma as an example. If you are going to borrow the ideas of the Balanced Scorecard, remember to understand the basics, know your present situation intimately and then apply what makes sense in your case. It is not about having a scorecard; it is about being someone who keeps an eye on your key organizational assets. The scorecard is one method. You may decide to use a scorecard or maybe you will come up with a better idea.

Every situation is unique. Perhaps there are assets other than the four we listed that you can ill afford to lose. Perhaps you have a technology like the fuelerator that is a competitive advantage for your organization. The key is to think broadly about how you obtain your results and to make sure you take care of the resources that provide those results. The real trick is to renew the resource before you hit a barrier and run out of whatever it is that delivers your results.

WHERE IS THAT CRYSTAL BALL?

One part of renewal is to plan and look ahead, to anticipate possible outcomes — not only the best, but also the worst. The example above about needing another factory is a good example of looking ahead. To keep lack of manufacturing capacity from being a barrier, the planning and construction has to start well before the company needs the capacity. Someone must not only anticipate that possibility but also commit resources to the thought. There is risk to that decision, as there is risk to not making it.

One of my managers once reminded me when I was being too conservative, *"If you wait until you have all the information, it is not a decision, it is just a fact.*

I am paying you to make decisions." And, by implication, he was paying me to take some risks.

MURPHY WAS AN OPTIMIST

As an engineer I was taught the art of worst-case circuit design. I designed circuits to perform adequately, even if we got the worst breaks from Mother Nature and from the components we used — simultaneously. This approach leads to the thinking in many engineers' heads, *"Plan for the worst and hope for the best."* Worst case design yields very robust electronics.

Unfortunately some of us bring that helpful concept for circuit design into the rest of our lives and we become risk averse: conveyors of facts rather than makers of decisions. This becomes a variation on the problem of growth forever. If things are going okay, just keep doing more of what you've been doing. Renewal may involve change. Renewal itself becomes a risk that some people don't want to take. But not renewing your resources may be the riskiest strategy of all.

SO WHAT?

Our organizations and the people in them are addicted to the urgent. Speed is God. Time is the devil. Fueled by the latest technology, everyone is available 24-7. Take a look in airports or, worse yet, look at people driving cars. Every third person has something in her ear or is talking to the air. They are constantly in do mode.

A friend of mine recently showed me how product development cycles have dramatically decreased over the last 15 years. Cycle time is a competitive advantage. Toyota, up the road from me in Georgetown, Kentucky, builds a Camry in under a minute. How cool is that? Nevertheless, as one of Toyota's managers said to me, *"If we are not careful, we will begin to try to fit our human interactions into the same small increments of time that we use to build the car. That will not work."*

Attention Deficit Disorder is an issue for schoolchildren and some adults, but the organizational equivalent is the wired multi-tasker with a huge sense of urgency, climbing the organizational ladder two steps at a time, complete with a corner office with a view, chest pains and a couple of divorces.

This need for speed permeates not only our organizations but also our lives, until both are out of balance. There is a natural cycle of action and reflection to the world. It takes both to complete the cycle. Yin Yang. Plan and Do, Check and Act. Use and renew.

This principle of renewal applies at every level, from a single sentient being up to the planet. In this book we've been focused on organizations. I'm convinced that an organization created with attention to and belief in the need for renewing all its aspects, as opposed to "use 'em up and throw 'em out," will be more durable, sustainable and competitive.

COMMON ORGANIZATIONAL RESOURCES

Some organizations get out of balance by putting too much emphasis on some types of resources while undervaluing others. This table puts on Hartman's glasses to list a number of systemic, extrinsic and intrinsic resources. Using these three divisions may help you recognize more of your own key assets and resources.

1. Systemic
   - systems, policies, rules, processes
   - knowledge, strategies, hierarchy, authority
   - vision of the future
   - clear mission

2. Extrinsic
   - products and services, work activities, projects, good work to do
   - materials and equipment, buildings, furniture and fixtures, computers, machines, productive meetings, training events, teams, social events, celebrations, awards, recognition
   - financial base, feedback for improvement
   - performance measures (dashboard)

3. Intrinsic
   - relationships between people
   - customer good will, encouragement, trust, ethics
   - loving the work, discretionary energy of the people
   - feeling cared about (I matter) as an employee

Now What

1. Experiment with a Balanced Scorecard in your own organization, or in your own personal life.
   a. What are your most important "bottom lines" or assets?
   b. On a scale of 0 = empty, 10 = full How would you rate each one?

2. Are you balancing use with renew? If one of your assets needs renewal, what one thing could you do to improve that resource?

3. Are you experiencing a Limits To Growth pattern in your life? Perhaps you have hit a plateau in your exercise program and are not seeing the progress you'd like. Or you aren't being intellectually challenged and haven't learned anything new lately. You may be experienced in your job. But, do you have ten years' experience or one year's experience ten times?

4. Notice what might be limiting your growth. What resource is being constrained? What could you do to "remove the brake" from that part of the system?

5. What will your Page say about taking care of assets and resources?

THE PAGE

Our work with clients is based on the following assumptions. Everyone does not hold these beliefs. We list them so people we work with will know what to expect from us.

ABOUT INDIVIDUALS:

+ Each individual is unique. He or she values ideas, things and people differently and responds to challenges differently. When individuals work together these differences can create chaos or synergy.
+ People choose their behavioral responses to what happens to them and are therefore responsible for their own behavior. They choose the best behavior they can think of based on internal and external motivation and their abilities. This behavior may or may not be effective.
+ Most people want to do well and succeed. They should have control over how they do their work, and understand why they do their work.
+ Leadership resides in every person. It is not reserved just for executives and managers.

ABOUT THE CULTURE:

+ A high-trust working environment will create better short and long-term results than a low-trust working environment.
+ People need feedback from processes, customers, suppliers and employees of an organization so they can improve. Facts, data and the scientific method provide feedback. Judgment and blame are not feedback.
+ An organization is an interdependent system. Competition within a culture creates winners and losers, artificial scarcity and loss. It does not help the organization. Competition between independent organizations is acceptable.

ABOUT ORGANIZATIONS:

+ Every organization is perfectly designe̶ ̶ ̶ ̶ ̶ ̶ ̶ ̶ ̶ ̶ ̶e of over 85% of the problems experienced ̶ ̶ ̶ ̶ ̶ ̶ ̶ ̶ ̶gies, structure, policies, procedures, etc. an̶ ̶ ̶ ̶ ̶ ̶ ̶ ̶
+ Organizations and individuals grow̶ ̶ ̶ ̶ ̶ ̶ ̶ ̶care of and improve the assets and reso̶ ̶ ̶ ̶ ̶ ̶ ̶ ̶ ̶ ̶ ̶ ̶ ̶ ̶by the stakeholders.

> *An organization stays in existence because all stakeholders, including customers, suppliers, employees, owners and the community are willing and able to continue the relationship.*

+ *An organization stays in existence because all stakeholders, including customers, suppliers, employees, owners and the community are willing and able to continue the relationship.*

Organizations as Parts of a larger System

CHAPTER 9

The Page

An organization stays in existence because all stakeholders, including customers, suppliers, employees, owners and the community are willing and able to continue the relationship.

Show Me The Money

When I ask *"What is the purpose of a business"* one of the most frequent answers is *"To make money for the stockholders."*

For me that answer is not so much wrong as it is insufficient. An organization needs money to function: it is like air for humans. We need air and can't survive very long without it. And yet, if asked about your purpose for being on the planet, you would probably not say *"To be a breather."* Doesn't the same reasoning apply to organizations? Yes, an organization needs money to continue its work. No margin, no mission. But is that its main and only reason for being? Is its purpose to just be a taker?

People who vote for "make money for the stockholders" are saying, in essence, take care of the money and everything else will take care of itself. There are similar camps, illustrated by books, articles and speakers. Some say, *"If you take care of the customers, everything else will take care of itself."* There is some truth in that. Others say, *"Take care of the employees like they were your finest customer and they will take care of the customers and everything will be fine."* There is also some truth in that. Organizations' reasons for being are not as simple as any one of these ideas.

Once again the quote attributed to Albert Einstein comes to my mind: *"Everything should be made as simple as possible, but no simpler."*

Analysis involves understanding something by examining its parts. Synthesis involves understanding something by seeing how it fits into a larger picture — seeing it as a part of something bigger. To stay in existence, an organization must coexist with larger systems. What makes organizations successful enough to stay in business within larger systems is not a one-dimensional problem.

TO OR IS HUMAN

In my engineering days some of the most fun I had at work was to design electronic logic circuits. In those early days before entire computers were available on one chip, we built our own electronic packages using a few simple circuits. We connected these little digital Legos together to make whatever we wanted. The basic circuit building blocks were AND gates and OR gates.

When working in digital binary logic, a gate is at one of two states (binary). It is either ON or OFF. An AND gate is ON when all of its inputs — the electrical signals that are wired to the input points of this gate from other circuits — are ON. The OR gate is similar, but different. The OR gate is ON when any of its inputs is turned on. Here endeth the digital logic lesson.

So what? It seems to me sometimes we treat a situation as an OR when it is an AND. For example, let's say my wife and I are deciding where to go for dinner. We narrow it down to four choices that will work for either of us; call them A, B, C and D. We pick one. We eat. Either A, or B, or C, or D worked. In digital logic terms, choosing a place for dinner is an OR decision.

Let's say over dinner we decide to have a party next month. Now we've got a number of decisions to make such as where to have it, whom to invite, what to serve, etc. Call these decisions X, Y and Z. That party is not going to happen until all three of these inputs, along with others, are decided. In digital logic terms, party planning = AND.

Like an AND gate that is a part of a larger complex circuit, an organization is a part of a larger interdependent system. Its "inputs" include but are not limited to customers, suppliers, employees and the various entities in the surrounding community. If any of these entities either cannot or will not continue in relationship with the organization, the organization goes out of existence. The organization needs all of them.

To put it another way, as we discussed in the competition chapter, some situations are independent and others are interdependent. An organization exists in a larger interdependent and symbiotic system. It affects others and others affect it.

How does this happen in reality? Some of the more obvious ways include:

- Another competitor offers a better deal to the customers. (Customer orders input goes to OFF).
- Raw material prices rise; causing a subcontractor to raise the prices of parts sold to the organization, making the supplier unable to provide parts at a competitive price. (Supplier goes to OFF).
- The Enron Effect (greed and corruption) causes the court to decide that the organization does not get to stay in business. (Legal system goes to OFF).
- Poor treatment from the organization makes it not worthwhile for customers and perhaps suppliers, to do business with the organization. (Customers and/or suppliers go to OFF).

I'm sure you can add many more examples. Perhaps some of these would not be fatal problems. Perhaps the corporation could rearrange itself to continue functioning, but in a somewhat different structure. Nevertheless, corporations today do not, on average, last as long as human beings. As Ari DeGeus points out in his book *The Living Company*, the organization is a relatively recent social construct and is still at a very early stage of evolution. Perhaps as we learn more about how to develop, organize and sustain companies the average one will outlive the average human.

WHAT IS YOUR PURPOSE?

I don't think the purpose of companies is just to make money. That begs the question, *"What is the purpose of organizations?"*

Dr. Deming was famous — or notorious — for beginning his conversations with corporate CEOs by asking them, *"What is your purpose?"* They would at first dismiss it as a dumb question. Most thought they were in business to provide a product or service and make money for the stockholders. Then as the management team would consider that question over a period of time, the answers tended to change. The purpose becomes something more — something worthy of investing the time and energy of all those involved in the venture.

I believe Dr. Deming asked this question because he knew that a common purpose is the unifying force that focuses and aligns people toward a common goal. To quote Dr. Viktor Frankl, Austrian psychiatrist and Holocaust survivor *"Those who have a 'why' to live can bear with almost any 'how.'"*

Without this common unifying force, each part of an organization creates its own unaligned mini-purpose. For example, Finance thinks its purpose is to save money. Research thinks its purpose is to create innovative new ideas. Manufacturing thinks its purpose is to build products. The organization becomes fragmented with independent parts. I heard someone describe their company as a loose affiliation of warring tribes.

In chapter seven I mentioned *The Nun and The Bureaucrat.* A great example of the power of common purpose is found in that book on page 18.

"Among the hospitals we studied in this book, the most crucial awareness they developed was that, amid all the complexity and rapid changes happening in health care, they had, paradoxically, 'forgotten' or 'lost' the patient. ...until they made the patient's needs and patient care their unifying purpose, they would never become a true system."

WE HAVE MET THE ENEMY

Thinking about their unifying purpose caused the hospital staff and leaders to rethink how they conducted their business. As people think about the unifying purpose of their organizations, they expand their definition of who is "us." At first, "us" is limited to their area or department or division. Then they see that they are one interdependent part of the larger organization. One more step up and they see their organization as an interdependent part of a larger community system and perhaps, using the same logic, their purpose should encompass that system. By now, the idea that their purpose is to make money for the stockholders looks too small. They have become more than that.

Every major spiritual tradition teaches that we are all a part of something larger. That something larger goes by different names, but the underlying concept is the same. I believe it is the same for organizations. Organizations belong to something larger. Call it what you will.

Once you connect that dot the question becomes *"Where do you draw the boundary around 'us'?"* Is "us" just the officers of the corporation? In that case we officers want to make sure we don't harm each other. Does "us" include all employees? What about our customers? Don't we say we are partners with our suppliers? What about them? Don't forget our neighbors who live near our plant. Shouldn't we include the animals and plants that share the air we use? Where do we stop and they start?

Who can we leave out of our circle? As the circle grows the purpose of the organization expands. What if our organization is connected to everything else? What if you and I are connected to everyone else? For me that is both reasonable and overwhelming.

It's Not Business, It's Personal

If we put on our Hartman glasses we can look at this idea of unifying purpose from three dimensions: systemic, extrinsic and intrinsic. Hartman's logic will take us to the same conclusion: that the purpose of an organization is much larger than to just make a profit.

From a systemic view of an organization — a view that includes concepts, ideas, rules, systems and mental constructs — the purpose of an organization is to make a profit while obeying the law. There are organizations that do and those that don't. Systemic valuation is black or white. It either is or it isn't. You are a member of the set or not. There is no gray area.

Hartman said that as we move from the systemic view to the extrinsic view, we take the systemic with us. That is, the extrinsic is a richer dimension, which includes the systemic and also contains the day-to-day realities of what *is*. The extrinsic view includes cause and effect, comparisons of good, better, best, etc. It is the dimension of practical thinking.

From the extrinsic point of view, the purpose of an organization is — in addition to making a profit and obeying the law — to produce high-quality, safe, useful products and services at a fair price and to provide value to our customers.

In their ads, Lexus refers to *"The relentless pursuit of perfection."* Perfection is a systemic mental concept. It is also part of the extrinsic dimension. Customers measure perfection extrinsically by the actual performance of the car.

But perfection is also intangible and emotional.

So a Lexus and many other products get evaluated by the tangible — the price, the quality, the reviews in auto magazines and by something more — something intangible.

In *The Elegant Solution — Toyota's Formula for Mastering Innovation*, Matthew May says, *"Lexus takes intangibles very seriously. There's probably nothing more intangible than perfection, which it pursues with passion."*

May goes on to give several examples of how Lexus captures the intangible.

Hartman calls this dimension of the intangible — of potential, of emotion, of the unique and personal — the intrinsic dimension. It is Hartman's richest dimension. It contains all of the extrinsic and systemic properties along with intangibles such as feelings, emotions, uniqueness and personality.

There is a Toyota television commercial that shows owners talking to their cars as if the cars were human, thereby valuing them intrinsically. The owners apologize to their cars. One young man even asks his Corolla, "You wanna go get some Chinese?"

The intrinsic dimension is, by definition, "soft and fuzzy." But it is important. It translates into real value in the mind of the consumer.

If I ask you to name a business, store, or car that you love, it will pop into your head immediately. For me, there is a local bookstore near my home that comes to mind. I can order books online from Amazon and sometimes I do. But there are days when I just want to go to this local place for a while. I support that bookstore, in part, because I enjoy being there. To that extent it has an intrinsic value for me and as a result, I am their customer.

When we were talking about individuals in Chapter 2, we looked at how motivation drives behavior. People buy things for many reasons, including intangible ones. As May says in *The Elegant Solution,*

"Intangible drivers of value get to the heart of what motivates purchase behavior. If you can answer the tougher questions of what tangibles do for the buyer — how speed improves life, what quality actually buys in the mind of the customer — you're entering the domain of intangible value. You transcend the mere economic transaction, because the emotional bonds that result are much stronger than the dollar exchange."

If you believe the role of business is only to make a profit, you might consider how the intrinsic dimension adds to that and enriches it.

Viewed intrinsically, the purpose of an organization is not only what we discussed in the other two dimensions — a transactional purpose — but also to be a unique member of the larger community, helping this community grow and prosper as no other entity can.

What does this concept allow for? What role can the organization uniquely fill? To me, *"What is the purpose of the organization?"* just became a spiritual question, in the sense of its being in the presence of and acting in accordance with, a larger entity.

So What?

Draw the circles of who is "us" and who is "them" in your life thoughtfully. Mark Gerzon, in his excellent book *Leaders Beyond Borders*, spells out a predictable five-step path to genocide. The first step, he says, is to define "the other" as someone different than you. If you draw a small circle, creating a lot of others, you may be drawing your own premature demise.

I believe we are all related, all interconnected and ultimately all interdependent on this fragile planet. We are all interdependent parts of one very large, incredibly complex system.

What is the purpose of an organization within this larger reality? Perhaps it is to be the glue that keeps us all connected. We learned in the chapter on competition that it does not make sense to compete with other parts of the same interdependent system. Perhaps in the near future the only way this planet will stay in existence is if all stakeholders realize the truth of our interdependence and choose to continue the relationship.

Now What?

Consider yourself within your organization or your family. Begin to think about how these entities function as parts of a larger system.

1. What can you do to nurture and grow the connections and relationships with those entities in the larger system? Consider your neighbors, your community, other departments in your organization, other organizations that interact with yours.

2. How would those around you describe you or your organization in a few words? What intangibles are your customers purchasing? Do others love doing business with you or being with you?

3. What will your Page say about you and organizations in the larger world?

4. Combine and review all your notes pertaining to your Page. Do they reflect your best thinking about organizations at this time?

Your Workshop Starts Now

CHAPTER 10

At the end of many of our workshops I comment to participants that, *"The workshop starts now."* What I mean is, unless people put what they have learned into practice in their own lives and organizations, the workshop has been at best just an interesting mental exercise. And now I say the same thing to you. Your workshop starts now.

Now what? You are probably tired of that question by now, especially if you have been answering this question at the end of each chapter. At some point we all answer the question, *"Now what?"* Even if we answer it by doing what we have always done.

You may remember from the coaching section in this book that *"What is your plan?"* is one of the four basic coaching questions. *"Now what?"* is another way to ask about your plan, your next steps. You may also remember that another of the coaching questions was to encourage self-evaluation by asking, *"Will what you are doing get you what you want?"*

Now is the time to coach yourself. If your first answer to *"Now what?"* is, *"Do nothing"* ask yourself if this strategy will get you what you want. Unless you want to more or less quit living, doing nothing is not a good option. Even if you are doing great right now, we have learned that nothing grows without limit. This may be the best time to look ahead at what might be your next constraint and begin taking action to avoid it before it is on top of you.

My intention in writing this book was to encourage the reader to begin both an internal dialogue with him or herself and an external dialogue with others in the organization about creating more meaningful work lives and healthier organizations. These divergent conversations will yield many different answers. Your own answers are the only ones that will count in the long run. We have learned that the most important conversations are usually about divergent topics that don't have one correct answer.

Take a lesson from Dr. Deming and begin by clarifying your purpose. What are you here to be? Take into consideration the unique individual that you are. Make sure your purpose is large enough to encompass all those you are interdependent with. Once you understand your purpose it will be easier to answer *"Now what?"*

Your *"Now what?"* needs to impact others in a positive way. From the "Win As Much As You Can" game we learned the flaw of "Xing" in an interdependent reality. Make sure your actions are based on positive intent for everyone.

Do not think that the only things worth doing are those that make headlines. Much can come from small actions taken at the right point in the system. And much can come from persistence, like water smoothing a rock in a creek over time.

Pick something in an organization that you are associated with. What needs to improve and probably won't if you don't take action? Form a plan. Think about how the ideas in this book can help you to create a plan. Do a small experiment. Be a curious researcher. Remember the Plan — Do — Check — Act cycle. Check the results of your experiment. Make changes as needed. Try another experiment. Gradually the system will improve.

Your workshop starts now. Go forth and do good.

REFERENCES

Introduction

Senge, Peter, et.al. *The Fifth Discipline Fieldbook, Strategies and Tools for Building A Learning Organization.* New York: Doubleday/Currency, 1994.

Chapter 1

Hartman, Robert S. *The Structure of Value: Foundations of Scientific Axiology.* Carbondale, Ill.: Southern Illinois University Press, 1967.

Mefford, David and Mera Mefford. *Personal Talent Skills Inventory Manual.* Phoenix: Target Training International Limited, 2006.

Spranger, Eduard. *Types of Men: The Psychology and Ethics of Personality.* Halle, Germany: M. Niemeyer, 1914; translation by P. J. W. Wigors; New York: G. E. Stechert Company, 1928.

Chapter 2

Bonnstetter, Bill J., Judy I. Suiter, and Randy J. Widrick. *The Universal Language DISC – A Reference Manual,* 11th ed. Phoenix: Target Training, International, 1984.

Chapter 3

McGregor, Douglas. "The Human Side of Enterprise." Article published in Adventures of Thought and Action, Proceedings of the Fifth Anniversary Convocation of the School of Industrial Management at MIT, Cambridge, Mass., 1957.

Gallwey, W. Timothy, *The Inner Game of Work*. New York: Random House, 1999.

Fisher, Roger, William Ury, and Bruce Patton. *Getting to Yes*. New York: Houghton Mifflin, 1981.

Chapter 4

Suzuki, Shunryu. *Zen Mind, Beginner's Mind*. Boston: Shambhala Publications, Inc., 2006. (Originally published in the USA: Weatherhill Publishers, 1973).

Greenleaf, Robert. *The Servant as Leader*. Westfield, Ind.: Robert K. Greenleaf Center, 1982.

Oshry, Barry. *Seeing Systems: Unlocking the Mysteries of Organizational Life*. San Francisco: Berret-Koehler Publishers, Inc., 1995.

Deming, W. Edwards. *Out of the Crisis*. Cambridge: Massachusetts Institute of Technology Center For Advanced Engineering Study, 1986.

DePree, Max. *Leadership Is An Art*. New York: Dell Publishing, 1990.

Chapter 5

Axelrod, Robert. *The Evolution of Cooperation*. New York: Basic Books, 1984.

Covey, Stephen R. *The 7 Habits of Highly Effective People*. New York: Simon and Schuster, 1989.

Goldratt, Eliahu. *The Goal*. Aldershot, UK: Gower Publishing, Ltd., 1986.

Suroweicki, James. *The Wisdom of Crowds: Why the Many Are Smarter Than The Few and How Collective Wisdom Shapes Business, Economies, Societies and Nations*. New York: Doubleday, 2004.

Chapter 6

Savary, Louis M., and Clare Crawford-Mason. *The Nun and The Bureaucrat: How They Found an Unlikely Cure For Today's Sick Hospitals*. San Francisco: Jossey-Bass and American Hospital Publishing, 2006.

Ernst, Ron. *RealTime Coaching: How to Make the Minute-By-Minute Decisions That Unleash The Power in Your People*. Carmel, Ind.: Leadership Horizons, LLC, 1999.

Chapter 7

Senge, Peter, et.al. *The Fifth Discipline Fieldbook, Strategies and Tools for Building A Learning Organization*. New York: Doubleday/Currency, 1994.

Chapter 8

Oestreich, Daniel K., and Kathleen D. Ryan. *Driving Out Fear in the Workplace: How to Overcome the Invisible Barriers to Quality, Productivity, and Innovation*, 2nd ed. San Francisco: Jossey-Bass, 1998.

Collins, Jim. *Good To Great* New York: Harper Collins, 2001.

Covey, Stephen R. *The 7 Habits of Highly Effective People*. New York: Simon and Schuster, 1989.

Kaplan, Robert, and David Norton. *The Balanced Scorecard: Translating Strategy Into Action*. Boston: Harvard Business School Press, 1993.

Chapter 9

DeGeus, Ari. *The Living Company: Habits For Survival in a Turbulent Business Environment*. Boston: Harvard Business School Press, 1997 and 2002.

Gerzon, Mark. *Leaders Beyond Borders*. Boulder, Colo.: Mark Gerzon, 2003.

May, Matthew E. *The Elegant Solution – Toyota's Formula for Mastering Innovation*. New York: Free Press, a division of Simon and Schuster, Inc., 2007.

Savary, Louis M., and Clare Crawford-Mason. *The Nun and The Bureaucrat: How They Found an Unlikely Cure For Today's Sick Hospitals*. San Francisco: Jossey-Bass and American Hospital Publishing, 2006.

Printed in the United States
137780LV00003B/1/P

9 781883 589882